I0393709

UNDERSTANDING BITCOIN:
The Liberty Lover's Guide to the Mechanics & Economics of Crypto-Currencies

By

Silas Barta
and
Robert P. Murphy

First Edition
December 2014

Table of Contents

Paperback Edition published 2015 by Skyler J. Collins
Visit: www.skylerjcollins.com

ISBN-13: 978-1505819786
ISBN-10: 1505819784

UNDERSTANDING BITCOIN:

The Liberty Lover's Guide to the
Mechanics & Economics of Crypto-Currencies

I. Introduction

This booklet is intended as a guide for the liberty lover on the subject of Bitcoin, which is the first and most popular of a new type of financial instrument called "crypto-currencies." Although Bitcoin is a fascinating subject in its own right, regardless of its possible political implications, it would be naïve to pretend that the public interest in Bitcoin today is *merely* one of commercial application and/or intellectual curiosity.[1] Just as the development of the Internet has had a tremendous impact on the prospects for liberty, today's ideological proponents of Bitcoin hope that Satoshi Nakamoto's solution to the "double-spending" problem in a decentralized payment system heralds a new tool in the struggle against oppressive States. In this respect, the appeal of Bitcoin is that—by its very nature—it cannot be commandeered by powerful third parties, which means that it is forever secure against unpredictable inflation.

In the case of the Internet, the liberty lover doesn't have to know exactly *how* it functions to appreciate its potential. The same is true for Bitcoin: Individuals can buy and sell with bitcoins, without having the slightest idea of what's really going on. However, to fully appreciate the beauty of Bitcoin—and to defuse some of the

---

[1] For a discussion of the ideological motivations among many of those who developed the architecture of Bitcoin, see Michael Goldstein's talk at the March 2014 Texas Bitcoin conference, posted here: https://www.youtube.com/watch?v=hPY-5SR-jPQ. More generally, see the literature compilation at the Satoshi Nakamoto Institute here: http://nakamotoinstitute.org/literature/.

December 2014

more popular objections to it—one must learn at least the basics of public key cryptography.

In this guide, we will serve both types of reader, giving intuitive explanations that provide the "big picture" of Bitcoin's economics but in separate sections we will delve into the actual mechanics of Bitcoin for the reader wanting to know more. At any point in this guide, if you the reader begin to feel overwhelmed by the technical details, we urge you to skip ahead to the next section. So long as you at least give each of the sections a chance, we are confident you will walk away understanding the mechanics and economics of Bitcoin much better than at the start.

Before diving in, let us offer three caveats that we urge readers to remember as they work through this guide:

➔ *We are NOT recommending Bitcoin as an investment.* Rather, we are describing its operation as a currency and a payment system, both in terms of the cryptography and the economics. We want to teach readers *how Bitcoin works.* Whether the exchange value of individual bitcoins (quoted in terms of other currencies for example) will rise or fall in the coming years is not our concern in this guide.

➔ In this guide, we will refer to Bitcoin specifically, but much of what we write is applicable to crypto-currencies more generically. We definitely believe that some form of Bitcoin-like currencies are now here to stay, but it is entirely possible that future developments will render the actual Bitcoin protocol obsolete, and that humans in the year (say) 2050 will use a more advanced crypto-currency that is superior to Bitcoin.

➔ Anyone is free to distribute and maintain copies of this guide. We merely ask that proper attribution be given to the original authors (Barta and Murphy). The guide will constantly be a work in progress; we welcome constructive feedback, and readers should check to see that they have the latest version, available at:

December 2014

http://understandingbitcoin.us/. We have made the PDF available to the world, and ask those who benefit from it to consider a Bitcoin donation (details at the end of the guide).

II. Why Do We Need Privately Created Money?

We the authors of this guide are extremely skeptical of the modern State, and consider it a major threat to both civil and financial liberties. The most obvious pitfall of State-issued money is the danger of hyperinflation, such as occurred in the German Weimar Republic between the World Wars, or in Zimbabwe in our times. Yet even moderate inflation entails the systematic transfer of wealth from the people holding the currency (or other assets denominated in it) to the institutions given the power to create new money. Proponents of this system sometimes argue that wages and prices adjust to make it all a wash, but consider: If someone offered *you* a printing press that could make legal tender notes, wouldn't you see how that would slant things in your favor?

Indeed, the State—and the banking interests with which it is allied—guard their money monopoly precisely *because* it is so lucrative. When the State wants to spend more than it can raise through taxes and private loans, it is quite convenient to cover its budget deficit through the creation of new money. To be sure, things are much more subtle these days than when rulers long ago would "debase" their coinage by adding in base metals,[2] but the end result is the same: Central governments are able to spend more—on both welfare and warfare—than their subjects would ever support through open taxation and private lending, because the central banks are waiting in the wings to issue new money and absorb the government debt. All the pretty rules enshrined in formal constitutions are rather toothless when the central government can, within broad limits, create money at will.

Yet there is another grave problem with State-controlled money. In our modern, State-sponsored system, new money enters the economy through the banking

---

[2] For a comprehensive explanation of modern-day currency debasement and deficit finance, see Robert P. Murphy, "The Fed as Giant Counterfeiter," February 1, 2010 Mises Daily article, available at: https://mises.org/library/fed-giant-counterfeiter.

sector. This means that the monetary inflation doesn't push up prices uniformly. Instead, *particular* prices are distorted first, and only gradually does the economy adjust to the increase in the quantity of money.

Specifically, *interest rates* are pushed artificially low during a period of excessive monetary inflation, pouring into the economy through the credit markets. Intuitively, the central bank and commercial banks create more money in the very act of issuing new loans. The only way to push these loans out to the public is to lower their price, in other words to cut the interest rate.

Here we're not offering any novel analysis; this is literally the textbook description of how modern central banks use "open market operations" to inject new reserves into the banking system, which the private commercial banks then pyramid into the creation of more money by the magic of the "multiplier." Conventional analysis agrees that the central bank can push down interest rates by creating new money in this fashion. The only difference is, the conventional analysis says *this is a beneficial practice* when the economy is in a slump.

In contrast, we subscribe to the theory of business cycles developed by the Austrian economist Ludwig von Mises and his disciple, Nobel laureate Friedrich Hayek. In the Mises-Hayek view, the artificially low interest rates aren't doing the economy any favors. Rather, they simply communicate faulty information—send a bad signal— and cause entrepreneurs to embark on projects that cannot be financed with genuine savings. The low interest rates thus *appear* to "cure" a recession and restore prosperity, but it's an illusion: The central bank's practices merely blow up another bubble that will eventually burst. The United States and Europe saw a great illustration of this process when the dot-com bubble of the late 1990s was replaced by the housing bubble of the mid-2000s.[3]

---

[3] There are several books that the reader can pursue to learn more on these topics, depending on the particular area of interest. For example see Richard Ebeling (ed.) [1978] 1996, *The Austrian Theory of the Trade Cycle and Other* Essays, available at:

For many people, the response of the Federal Reserve (and other central banks around the world) to the financial crisis of 2008 underscored the flaws with the present, State-dominated system, when enormous amounts of new money were (electronically) created in order to bail out institutions deemed "too big to fail." Beyond the dubious economic merits behind such actions, the fact that they were quite secretive—with Ben Bernanke for example testifying to Congress in December 2008 that it would defeat the purpose of the Fed's actions if he were to divulge the beneficiaries of its "extraordinary" lending operations [4] —confirmed for many skeptics that the modern entanglement of money and the State benefits the elite at the expense of the general public.

Examples of Private Money, Before Bitcoin

The previous section summarized some of the main concerns of people who reject the State's monopoly in money. Rather than let the State provide the money, the natural alternative is for private citizens to produce it.

Originally, the market produced *commodity* money, in which the item that the community used as money, was also a regular commodity that was useful in trade. Historically, many commodities served as money at different times and places, including cattle, salt, shells, and even cigarettes. However, especially as industrial

---

https://mises.org/library/austrian-theory-trade-cycle-and-other-essays; Murray Rothbard, 2008, *The Mystery of Banking*, available at:
http://mises.org/library/mystery-banking-1; and Carlos Lara and Robert P. Murphy, 2010, *How Privatized Banking Really Works*, available at:
http://consultingbyrpm.com/uploads/HPBRW.pdf. Note that full bibliographical citations are available at the end of this guide.
[4] See for example the Bloomberg article by Mark Pittman, "Fed Refuses to Disclose Recipients of $2 Trillion," on December 12, 2008, available at:
http://www.bloomberg.com/apps/news?pid=newsarchive&sid=aGvwttDayiiM, which refers to Bloomberg News' November 7, 2008 Freedom of Information Act request, and the December 10 Congressional hearing. The Fed's official response was that disclosing the names of the financial institutions accessing the Fed's new emergency programs would cause investors' to dump these firms and hence undermine the whole rationale of the programs.

capitalism swept the world in the relatively free-trade era of the 1800s, the advanced nations settled on gold and silver as the commodity monies of choice.

Typically, critics of State-issued "fiat" money (which means money that is not backed up by any other asset) have longed for a return to "hard" commodity money, such as gold. Just to clarify, people who champion "gold money" don't necessarily envision people buying houses with hunks of yellow metal. Rather, they imagine a society in which the underlying unit of money is indeed a certain weight of gold, where no single institution is "in charge" of the money supply because there are miners spread out all over the globe. Yet even within that framework, private mints could stamp recognizable (and hard to counterfeit) gold coins, and private commercial banks could accept deposits of physical gold in exchange for issuing debit cards and checkbooks to make large purchases in the gold money more convenient.[5]

Some economists, such as Benjamin Klein and Nobel laureate Friedrich Hayek, even went so far as to embrace the use of fiat monies, so long as they were issued in a competitive marketplace.[6] In other words, rather than having the people of the world choose among the dollar issued by the Federal Reserve, the euro issued by the European Central Bank, the yen issued by the Bank of Japan, and so on, some economists imagined private companies issuing their own (unbacked) notes and electronic claims, with the reputation and "monetary policies" of the individual companies giving customers a much more appetizing suite of choices in currency. After all, having Apple and Microsoft compete in software certainly yields much

---

[5] For an understandable yet thorough introduction to the history of money and the restoration of gold as money, see Murray Rothbard's 1962 *The Case for a 100 Percent Gold Dollar*. For a discussion of the historical gold standard and private mints, see George Selgin's 2011 *Good Money*.

[6] The most famous example is Hayek's 1976 *The Denationalisation of Money*. For a discussion of his vision, see Robert P. Murphy, 2005, "Hayek's Plan for Private Money," available at: http://mises.org/library/hayeks-plan-private-money. However an earlier discussion is Benjamin Klein's 1974 "The Competitive Supply of Money" published in the *Journal of Money, Credit, and Banking,*

better results for consumers than letting (say) the governments of the U.S. and Russia produce all of the computer code, so why not do the same with money? Perhaps privately-issued fiat money could retain the ostensible advantages of fiat money (such as economizing on scarce physical commodities) while avoiding the obvious pitfalls of State-issued fiat money.

Bitcoin Enters the Scene

In this context, one can appreciate the confusion and excitement that Bitcoin generated as wider circles of first tech enthusiasts and then more ideologically motivated people learned of its properties and promise.[7]

On the one hand, Bitcoin seemed to be another example of a privately issued fiat currency—of the kind economist Benjamin Klein had discussed as early as 1974— with a digital twist for the Internet age. However, Bitcoin was much more than that. As the very title of Nakamoto's famous white paper announces, Bitcoin was a cash *system*, and moreover one that was *peer-to-peer*.

This is a huge advance over the conventional understanding of privately issued money. For example, in Hayek's vision each currency would still be issued by a particular institution, which could (in principle) easily violate whatever pledges it had made to the community concerning the rate of growth in the money supply. To be sure, private competition and the other mechanisms of contract enforcement would make private firms far more trustworthy than States, but nonetheless Hayek's plan (and those like it) relied on *trust*.

---

[7] In November 2008 Satoshi Nakamoto (which may be a pseudonym) published online the famous white paper, "Bitcoin: A Peer-to-Peer Electronic Cash System," available at: https://bitcoin.org/bitcoin.pdf. In January 2009 Nakamoto mined the first 50 bitcoins in what is called the "genesis block."

In contrast, because it is built on a peer-to-peer framework, the Bitcoin protocol dispenses with trust altogether. As we will explain in careful detail in the following sections, *nobody* is "in charge" of Bitcoin, so there's nobody with the *power* to break its rules and violate the public's trust. It is this element of Bitcoin that allows it to serve both as a unit of payment but also as a *system to move* payments around the globe, with incredible ease.

Once the truly revolutionary aspect of Bitcoin sinks in, it is hard not to be awed by the tremendous possibilities. Indeed, some enthusiasts mark the advent of the "blockchain"—a Bitcoin term that we will carefully explain in subsequent chapters—as a significant technological and cultural milestone in the development of the human race.[8]

In this guide, we focus on explaining the nuts and bolts of Bitcoin, but we wanted to set the stage properly to understand the importance of our discussion. Armed with a thorough understanding of how Bitcoin works, the reader can turn to other speakers and writers to consider the implications of Bitcoin (and related crypto-currencies) for the future.

---

[8] In libertarian circles, one of the biggest champions of Bitcoin in this respect is Jeffrey Tucker. See his forthcoming *Bit By Bit: How P2P [Peer to Peer] Is Freeing the World*.

December 2014

III. How Bitcoin Works: Explaining the Protocol

"Bitcoin" encompasses two related but distinct concepts. First, individual bitcoins (lowercase-b) are units of (fiat)[9] digital currency. Second, the Bitcoin (uppercase-B) protocol governs the decentralized network through which thousands of computers across the globe maintain a "public ledger"—known as the *blockchain*—that keeps a fully transparent record of every authenticated transfer of bitcoins from the moment the system became operational in early 2009. In short, Bitcoin encompasses both (1) an unbacked, digital currency and (2) a decentralized, online payment system.

According to its official website: "Bitcoin uses peer-to-peer technology to operate with no central authority; managing transactions and the issuing of bitcoins is carried out collectively by the network."[10] Anyone who wants to participate can download the Bitcoin software to his or her own computer and become part of the network, engaging in "mining" operations and helping to verify the history of transactions.

To fully understand how Bitcoin operates, one needs to learn the subtleties of public-key cryptography, which we discuss in subsequent sections. For now, we focus instead on an analogy that captures the economic *essence* of Bitcoin, while avoiding the need for new terminology.

---

[9] Some Bitcoin enthusiasts may object to our classification of it as a "fiat" currency, because the Bitcoin network is completely voluntary and doesn't rely on State-enforced legal tender laws or other methods of suppressing competition. However, in monetary economics the term "fiat" has a very precise meaning, under which bitcoins would qualify. (See Ludwig von Mises' *The Theory of Money and Credit* for a scholarly treatment.) In particular, it is simply not true that the State can merely declare "through fiat" that something is money. In our judgment, it is more important for the beginner to understand that there is no other commodity or asset "backing up" bitcoins—and in this sense it is a fiat currency—rather than avoiding the possibly negative connotations from our use of a term that is usually reserved for low-quality money issued by modern States.

[10] See: http://Bitcoin.org.

Understanding the Basics of Bitcoin With an Analogy[11]

Imagine a community where the money is based on the integers running from 1, 2, 3, ..., up through 21,000,000. At any given time, one person "owns" the number **8**, while somebody else "owns" the number **34,323**, and so on.

In this setting, Bill wants to buy a car from Sally, and the price sticker on the car reads, "Two numbers." Bill happens to be in possession of the numbers **18** and **112**. So Bill gives the two numbers to Sally, and Sally gives Bill the car. The community recognizes two facts: The title to the car has been transferred from Sally to Bill, and Sally is now the owner of the numbers **18** and **112**.

In this fictitious community, an industry of thousands of accountants maintains the record of ownership of the 21 million integers. Each accountant keeps an enormous ledger in an Excel file. The columns run across the top, from 1 to 21 million, while the rows record every transfer of a particular number. For example, when Bill bought the car from Sally, the accountants who were within earshot of the deal entered into their respective Excel files, "Now in possession of Sally" in the next available row, in the columns for **18** and **112**. In these ledgers, if we looked one row above, we would see, "Now in the possession of Bill" for these two numbers, because Bill owned the numbers before he transferred them to Sally.

Besides documenting any transactions that happen to be within earshot, the accountants also periodically check their own ledgers against those of their neighbors. If an accountant ever discovers that his neighbors have recorded transactions for *other* numbers (i.e., for deals for which the accountant in question was *not* within earshot), then the accountant fills in those missing row entries in the columns for those numbers. Therefore, at any given time, there are thousands of

---

[11] The material in this section is adapted from Robert P. Murphy, 2013, "The Economics of Bitcoin," available at:
http://www.econlib.org/library/Columns/y2013/Murphybitcoin.html.

accountants, each of whom has a virtually complete history of all 21 million numbers.

In our analogy, we are dealing with the end state, after all of the bitcoins have been "mined." This will occur at some point after the year 2100, when (virtually) all of the 21 million bitcoins will be in the hands of the public.[12] In the real world, when people want to buy something using Bitcoin, they transfer their ownership of a certain amount of bitcoins to other people, in exchange for goods and services. This transfer is effected by the network of computers performing computations and thereby changing the "public key" to which the "sold" bitcoins are assigned. This is analogous to the accountants in our story entering a new person's name in the column for a given integer.

Where Does Cryptography Come In? The Problem of Anonymous Owners

First, to clarify: Though you may often hear the term "encryption" in this context, Bitcoin doesn't actually use encryption, as that doesn't address the relevant problem here. We don't want to *hide* the transaction messages; rather, we want to *authenticate* them.[13]

---

[12] Strictly speaking, the total quantity of mined bitcoins will never *quite* reach 21 million; the protocol ensures that eventually the reward for mining a new block will be rounded down to literally zero bitcoins (sometime around the year 2140). But it is currently projected that by the year 2108, mining from that point onward will only bring into circulation ever smaller fractions of the 21 millionth bitcoin; see https://en.bitcoin.it/wiki/Controlled_supply#Projected_Bitcoins_Long_Term. Another complication is that some (fractions of) bitcoins will be "lost" over the decades, as people die, or forget their private keys, and so on. Therefore, even though these (fractions of) bitcoins will have been mined, they will forever be inaccessible in transactions, making them effectively removed from the "quantity of bitcoins" available to the public. They will be economically equivalent to gold coins that went down with a ship and are sitting at the bottom of the ocean.

[13] The confusion may come from the fact that *both* encryption and authentication are topics contained in the field of cryptography. They are also "dual" to each other in that, in public key systems, the operation of signing a message is the same as decrypting one, and the operation of verifying a signature is the same as encrypting

Let us return to our fictitious world of Bill and Sally, where the money is based on publicly recognized "ownership" of the 21 million integers. Our story above had one glaring problem we need to address: How do the accountants *verify the identity* of the people who try to buy things with numbers? In our example, Bill wanted to sell **18** and **112** to Sally for her car.

Now Bill really *is* the owner of the numbers **18** and **112**; he can afford Sally's car, because she's asking "Two numbers" for it. (And by the way, in this community when people quote a price in terms of "numbers" everybody knows it means "between 1 and 21 million," because any integer outside this range is not considered legitimate money.) The accountants will verify, if asked, that Bill is the owner of those numbers; it says "Bill" in the last row which has an entry in it, under the "**18**" column and the "**112**" column in all of their ledgers.

But here's the problem: When the nearby accountants see Bill trying to buy the car from Sally, how do they know *that that human being actually IS the "Bill" listed in their ledgers?* There needs to be some way that the *real* Bill can demonstrate to all of the accountants that he is in fact the same guy referred to in their ledgers. To prevent fraudulent spending of one's money by an unauthorized party, this mechanism must be such that *only the real Bill* will be able to convince the accountants that he's the guy.

In the real world, *this* is where all of the complicated public/private key cryptography comes in. To reiterate, in later sections of this guide we *will* go over all of this material in as intuitive a way as we can. But at this stage, we want to provide a basic understanding of Bitcoin even for readers who really don't want to wade into such technical details.

---

a message. But to repeat, strictly speaking Bitcoin doesn't rely on encryption, even though many people often say that it does.

Unfortunately, at this point our story of Bill and Sally gets a little silly, because we haven't been able to come up with a good analogy for this aspect of the Bitcoin process. So without further ado, suppose the following is how the people in our fictitious world deal with the problem of matching the names in the accountants' Excel ledgers with real-world human beings:

Each time one of the numbers is transferred in a sale, the new owner has to invent a riddle that only he or she can solve. You see, the people in the community are clever enough to recognize the correct answer to the riddle *when they hear it*, but they are not nearly creative enough to *discover* the answer on their own.

For example, when Bill himself received the numbers **18** and **112** from his employer—Bill gets paid "two numbers" every month in salary—the accountants said to Bill:

"OK Bill, to protect your ownership of these two numbers, invent a riddle that we will associate with them. We will embed the riddle inside the same cell in our ledger as the name "Bill," in the columns under 18 and 112. Then, when you want to spend these two numbers, you tell us the answer to your riddle. We will only release these numbers to a new owner, if the person claiming to be "Bill" can answer the riddle. Keep in mind, Bill, that you might be on the other side of town, surrounded by accountants you have never seen before, when you want to spend these numbers. That's why our seeing you right now, isn't good enough. We need to put down a riddle in our ledgers, which will also be copied thousands of times as the information pertaining to this sale reverberates throughout the community, so that every accountant will eventually have "Bill" and your riddle, embedded in the correct cell in his or her ledger."

Bill thinks for a moment and then has an ingenious riddle. He tells the accountants, "When is a door not a door?" They dutifully write down the riddle, which then gets propagated throughout the community.

A few days later, some villain tries to impersonate Bill. He wants to buy a necklace that has a price tag of "one number." So the villain says to the accountants in earshot, "I'm Bill. I am the owner of **112**, as everyone can see; these spreadsheets are public information. So I transfer my ownership of **112** to this jeweler, in exchange for the necklace."

The accountants say, "OK Bill, just verify your identity. What is the solution to your riddle? Tell us, 'When is a door not a door?'"

The villain thinks and thinks, but can't come up with anything. He says, "When the door isn't a door!" The accountants look at each other, scratch their heads, and agree, "No, that's a dumb answer. That didn't solve the riddle." So they deny the sale; the villain is not given the necklace.

Now, a few weeks later, we are up to the point at which our story originally began, at the beginning of this chapter. The real Bill wants to buy Sally's car for "two numbers." He announces to the nearby accountants, "I am the owner of **18** and **112**. I verify this by solving my riddle: A door is not a door *when it's ajar.*"

The accountants all beam with delight! Aha! *That* is a good answer to the riddle. They agree this must be the real Bill, and allow the sale to go through. They write down "Sally" in the next-available rows in columns **18** and **112**, and then ask Sally to give them a new riddle, to which only Sally would know the answer.

Explaining the Relevance to Bitcoin, Once Again

Even though we had to strain the story a bit—since in reality, it would be pretty easy for someone to guess the solution to Bill's riddle—we think this is a decent analogy to how Bitcoin actually works. Without getting into the details, there is a way that the actual owner can perform an operation mathematically that can only be *reversed* with possession of a specific number. This special number is the "private key." In our story, the private key would be analogous to Bill's mental ability to solve his own riddle, and the actual solution to the riddle would be his "signature." In the real world, once given a "signature" that can only be generated by someone with the private key, the computers in the Bitcoin network recognize that the owner is legitimate. It would take thousands of years of computing power (with current technology) for an outsider to *guess* the private key and hence produce a "valid" signature. Even the NSA with its supercomputers thus couldn't transfer someone else's Bitcoins by "forging" a digital signature.[14]

One final twist of realism: In the real world, people don't need to use their actual names such as "Bill" to identify themselves as the owner of a particular Bitcoin. Instead, they can use any old identifier. This identifier is the "public key," which all can see. In our analogy, it would be as if Bill told the accountants, "Call me 'CoolKat' in your ledgers." Then, to prove that he was in fact "CoolKat," Bill would have to answer the riddle, just as before.

The reason many privacy advocates are so excited about this aspect of Bitcoin is that Bill can disguise how many numbers he possesses. He can slap the label "CoolKat" on **18** and **112**, but he can throw "JamesBondFan" on his other numbers **45** and **974**. So Bill owns four numbers total, but nobody else in the community—not even the accountants—would know this. As far as the records indicate, **18** and **112** are owned by "CoolKat," while "JamesBondFan" owns **45** and **974**. Nobody but Bill realizes that these point to the same human being.

---

[14] In reality, the danger is not that a rogue would be able to produce a "valid" signature without having the private key; that indeed would be virtually impossible. What *is* a realistic threat is that an entity with sufficient computational power relative to the entire Bitcoin network could go ahead and approve transactions even though the correct signature was not produced. This is what people mean by a "51% attack," and we deal with it in our discussion of mining pools.

"Mining" New Bitcoins

For simplicity, our analogy started with the 21 million units of currency already mined. However, in reality the process by which computers in the network verify transactions is intimately related to the increase in the quantity of bitcoins. When Bitcoin was first implemented in early 2009, computers in the network—dubbed "miners"—received 50 new bitcoins when performing the computations necessary to add a "block" of transactions to the public ledger. As of this writing, the reward has dropped to 25 new bitcoins per block, and the amount will continue to be halved every 210,000 blocks (which will predictably occur about every four years because the computational difficulty of the mining task is periodically calibrated to the recent computational power of the network). Eventually, probably around the year 2140, the number of new bitcoins awarded per block will be rounded down to zero, thus capping the total quantity of bitcoins in existence (at just under 21 million).[15]

In principle, the developer(s) of Bitcoin could have released all 21 million units of the currency immediately with the protocol.[16] Yet that would have almost certainly killed the project in its cradle. With the current arrangement—where the "mining" operations needed to keep the system running simultaneously yield new bitcoins to the machines performing the calculations—there is an incentive for people to devote their machines' processing power to the network (and for them to raise awareness of the new currency). If people want to pay fees on the side to expedite the verification of a Bitcoin transfer, they can do so, but (in this initial phase) the network eventually will get around to processing a transaction even if the parties involved have attached no extra fee. Such a feature is an ingenious way to encourage the widespread adoption of Bitcoin and help it "get off the ground."

---

[15] The projected quantity of bitcoins per mined block, as well as the total number of bitcoins mined to date, over time is available at the Bitcoin wiki: https://en.bitcoin.it/wiki/Controlled_Currency_Supply.

[16] As the software for Bitcoin is open to the public, others have created similar crypto-currencies ("altcoins"), and some of them release the units on a different schedule. Dogecoin in particular releases them without an upper bound.

December 2014

Kick It Up a Notch! Making the Analogies Harder But Closer to the Real Bitcoin

The above analogy of Bill buying a car from Sally was very intuitive while still giving a pretty good "big picture" understanding of what Bitcoin *is* and how it works as both a currency and payment system. However, in order to keep out any math our simple story ignored some important questions about the real-world implementation of such a system.

First of all, how do you get the riddle system to reliably work? How can you make it so that only one person can authorize the signing over of integers, while everyone else can verify it? And won't you run out of riddles?

Second, how do you resolve conflicting transactions without a central authority? If someone broadcasts two different valid messages claiming to send the same integer to two different people, how do you decide which transaction to keep and make official?

The first problem happens to be a long-solved one in cryptography, with a mature solution. It was around decades before Bitcoin. Let's review that first by walking through a simplified example of a "toy" digital signature scheme. Naturally, the math used in actual applications of cryptography is more complicated—and secure—but this toy example should get the general idea across.

To this end, we proudly present the Cow-Chicken Signature Scheme. You might remember a puzzle from school that went like this:

"A farmer has cows and chickens on his farm. In total, his animals have 5 heads and 16 feet. How many cows and how many chickens does he have?" (In case you forgot, chickens have 1 head and 2 feet, while cows have 1 head and 4 feet.)

In reality, most people would probably tackle this puzzle with algebra, and indeed these types of word problems are a great way to teach students how to set up equations involving "x" and "y." But to serve as an analogy for the cryptography used in Bitcoin, pretend that (for whatever reason) we can't use algebra, or any higher math, to solve our Cow-Chicken puzzle. Instead, we are only allowed to use the method of "guess and check": We simply guess the numbers of cows and chickens, then count up the corresponding numbers of heads and feet, and see if they match what the problem said.

You can see a certain asymmetry here: it's "easy" to go from cows and chickens to heads and feet. But given the heads and feet, it's "hard" to deduce the number of cows and chickens. In practice, you'll end up going through lots of "checks" before you eventually stumble upon the correct "guess."

Bear with us for one more wrinkle, and you'll see the obvious relevance to Bitcoin. Suppose that one person—let's call her Alice—actually *has* the formula that allows her to quickly convert heads and feet into the corresponding numbers of cows and chickens.[17] This formula is Alice's *private key*. Now remember, this is the "hard" direction, especially because we are pretending that for some reason, the general population doesn't know how to do algebra. It's easy for everybody to go the *other* way—turning the number of Cows and Chickens into the numbers of heads and feet—but it's hard "in your head" to go the opposite direction. In this environment, Alice—armed with the special formula—would seem to have a magical power. She alone could instantly take two numbers (of heads and feet) and spit out how many Cows and Chickens there must be. In contrast, everybody else would be sputtering around, guessing at the numbers of animals and then mentally "checking" to see if

---

[17] The formula, as it turns out, is: Cows = F/2 – H; Chickens = 2*H – F/2. Although it might seem silly, readers will probably "see" the point of this analogy better if they actually work through our specific example. To repeat, if we tell you that a farmer has 3 cows and 2 chickens, it's very easy to compute that this implies 5 total heads and 16 total feet. But if we instead had told you that a farmer has animals with a total of 5 heads and 16 feet, it would take most people several guesses to get the answer. Yet using the formulas above, the answer pops out instantly. The number of cows is (16/2) – 5 = 3, while the number of chickens is (2*5) – (16/2) = 2.

their guesses worked.

The specific math problem she uses—the fact that it's about cows and chickens with their corresponding number of heads and feet—is known as the *public key*, and also serves as an *address* to identify an account. Once formatted, Alice might announce her Bitcoin address as something like "1/4-1/2," which also tells you what math problem she knows the quick solution to. (Perhaps the community here has agreed to format their addresses as "first animal: heads/feet-second animal: heads/feet." That's why Alice writing "1/4-1/2" would let everyone familiar with this convention or *protocol* know that she was claiming to be able to quickly solve a Cow-Chicken problem, as opposed to a Cow-Spider problem.)

Putting It All Together

With our setup, we can now imagine how the whole system would work, in analogy to Bitcoin:

When Alice wants to sign a Bitcoin transaction, she has two important numbers: the amount of bitcoins she wants to transfer, and the address to which she wants to send them. She takes the transfer amount to be the number of heads, and the target address to be the number of feet. Then, her signature is just the corresponding number of cows and chickens, which she can easily compute using her private key (the secret formula). Assume she outputs the cows, then chickens, separated by a colon, like "8:2" for eight cows and two chickens.

To take a specific example, assume Alice wants to give 10 units to address 28. She first treats the 10 as the number of heads, and 28 as the number of feet. Now remember, to everyone else in the community, it's not obvious how to start with "10 heads, 28 feet" and transform it into the correct number of Cows and Chickens. But Alice, using her secret formula (i.e. private key), can quickly compute the number of cows as $28/2 - 10 = 4$ and chickens as $2*10 - 28/2 = 6$. So her signature is "4:6."

Then she broadcasts to the world, "I'm giving 10 units to address 28. My signature for this is 4:6." Even though it would have been very mentally taxing and time-consuming for people to *discover* the "4:6," they can very quickly *check it* to see if it works: Anybody who wants to verify Alice's purported signature can easily check that 4 cows and 6 chickens do indeed correspond to 10 heads and 28 feet. Bingo! Since only Alice is supposed to have the secret formula (private key) that generates a signature to go along with her public announcements of transferring units to recipient addresses, the public trusts that this particular announcement of, "I'm giving 10 units to address 28" is legitimately coming from Alice. Only she would have the ability to quickly discover the "4:6" signature, even though anybody else could quickly go the opposite direction to verify that it checked out.

We hope the silly Cow-Chicken example has already shed light on how Bitcoin works in the real world, but let's drive home the point by going through the necessary criteria of a signature we discussed before:

The Signature Can't Be Transferred Onto a Different Transaction

Part of the difficulty of using the term "signature" is that in everyday language, a person's signature is the same regardless of the document; you sign your name the same way, whether it's on the credit card payment stub at the restaurant or on the consent form at the doctor's office. However, in the context of digital signatures in public/private key cryptography, the "signature" does uniquely identify the signer, but the "signature" is itself dependent on the content of the message that it is authenticating.

To see what we mean, think about the transaction we described above. Suppose the scoundrel at address 28 sees how Alice "signed" her legitimate message to the network, telling it to transfer 10 units of her currency to address 28. Now that the scoundrel at 28 sees her "signature," couldn't he just send a *new* message, authorizing the transfer of (say) *12* units of Alice's currency to address 28, and pasting in her same "signature"? How would the network recognize that this request came from a fraud, and not the real Alice, if she has just publicly "signed" something?

The answer (to repeat) is that Alice's digital "signature" is *not* a static thing, like "John Hancock" made up of a bunch of 0s and 1s. On the contrary, the way the protocol works, Alice's legitimate signature will *be different*, depending on the transaction it is authenticating. In this case, people in the community would see a message purportedly from Alice announcing, "I'm giving 12 units to address 28. My signature is 4:6." Yet for those who bother to verify this announcement, they will find it doesn't "check" out. Specifically, they compute the number of heads and feet that correspond to 4 cows and 6 chickens, and get 10 and 28—not 12 and 28. They see that this announcement is invalid, and cannot trust that Alice actually sent it.

---

[18] Stick-figure comics made with the Comix I/O editor at http://cmx.io.

The signature is easy to verify ...

Since going from cows/chickens to heads/feet is easy, people can quickly check the validity of the signature.

... but hard to forge.

Since people (by assumption in our analogy, though not in the real world) can't do better than the guess-and-check technique, they have to guess a huge number of cow/chicken values until they find one that corresponds to the message for which they want to forge a signature. Alice doesn't have this problem: by knowing the private key (the quick formula) and keeping it secret, she's the only one that can generate these signatures so quickly and deftly.

Putting Together a Widely Used Signature System

In a widely-used system, we need to allow a huge number of people to join, while keeping separate addresses—and therefore, separate private and public keys. In the example above, Alice has "reserved" the math problem with cows and chickens—or rather, the two-animal math problem where one animal is of "type 1/4" (one head four feet) and the other is of type 1/2 (one head, two feet). Any newcomer must then pick "animals" with different "types." For the purposes of the system, the animal doesn't need to be one that exists on earth, as there are so few types under this system. So we would allow users to pick an imaginary "3/7" animal (3 heads, 7 feet), and so on, allowing for the creation of an unlimited number of addresses.

We also assume that users can pick an "animal pair" (which functions as a public key and address if you'll recall), and then a few seconds later, get the "private key" (special formula), while no one else does. Users can pick as many addresses as they like, without revealing how many they own.[19] From the perspective of the users, it looks the same whether Alice sends bitcoins from two addresses, or two different people each send from their own address.

How to Reach Agreement on the Transaction Order: Proof-of-Work Systems

While the above may seem clever, it's actually a long-running solution to the digital signature problem, and not the key innovation Bitcoin brought to the table. Rather, that would be its solution to the second problem we outlined earlier: How do you get everyone to agree on which transactions to include in the global ledger? Digital signatures, described above, ensure that you can prove a transaction was really authorized; they stop an outsider from spending someone else's currency. But what if someone signs two transfers of the same money (or same integer, to continue with our analogy) to two different people? After all, even if Jack the Scammer can correctly generate signatures for his addresses to prove that he genuinely issued a command to transfer bitcoins to another person, the community needs a way to check whether the specific bitcoins are Jack's to give in the first place! In other words, we also have to guard against a *legitimate owner* from spending his or her own currency more than once. This is known as the "double-spending problem."

Here is where Bitcoin's clever solution comes into play. For some background, we the authors of the present guide (Barta and Murphy) had always been interested in the theoretical possibility of privately issued currencies, but had assumed they would still need some trusted central party to be "the authority" on which transactions within its network were valid, and that competition between currencies would ensure that this power not be abused. But it turns out even this

---

[19] In the actual Bitcoin signature system, users pick a private key at random, and then follow a short process to find the corresponding public key/address. The space of keys is so large (2^{160}, or the square of the number of grains of sand on the earth) that users are astronomically unlikely to pick the same one, especially given that they don't know each others' private key and so can't deliberately pick one that's likely to match others'.

assumption is unnecessary: you can resolve currency and accounting disputes without a trusted third party. This is the true innovation embedded in Satashi Nakamoto's elegant white paper on Bitcoin. We describe the Bitcoin method below.

The Blockchain: Coordinating on the Same Transaction Record

In a sentence, the way that Bitcoin gets everyone to agree on a ledger is to have one rule in the protocol, what we can describe as:

Bitcoin's central trick: Of all the valid ledgers, use the one with the most proven work invested in it.

Of course, to someone new to the system, and to cryptography, this just raises more questions:

1) How do you know how much work was invested in something?
2) How do people invest work in the ledger?
3) Why do people invest work in the ledger at all?

Let's handle these questions in turn.

Proof of Work: The Guessing Game

First, an analogy: let's say you and a friend are playing a game where you try to guess your friend's number, which is somewhere between 1 and 1000 inclusive. Your friend secretly commits to a number in advance, and after each guess tells you whether that was the number. (Your friend only tells you "yes" or "no" after each guess, without giving any more information.)

On average, it will take you 500 guesses to win. So if you and your friend play a large number of times, we can assume your guess history roughly approximated this figure. In that sense, we can infer that the total number of guesses you must have made is about equal to 500 times your number of wins. So the game functions as a kind of "proof of work," similar to what Bitcoin uses: the fact that you were able to win X times is proof (if only statistical) that you made 500*X guesses.

Cryptographic Proof of Work: The Guessing Game With Scramblers

Cryptographic techniques allow you to play a similar game, involving what we'll call "Scrambler Functions" (in the jargon, cryptographically-secure one-way functions). These are functions that are easy to compute in one direction, but hard to invert. That is, given an input A and a scrambler function f(A), it's easy to compute f(A).

However, if you only know the output f(A), there's no way to find A except by guessing every possible input.[20]

These functions allow for the "crypto variant" of the guessing game. Instead of your friend picking a secret number, your friend just tells you his number, and the challenge for you is to find an input number that, when put through the Scrambler Function, results in your friend's number. It's every bit as hard as the original guessing game, but allows your friend to publish his number in advance for everyone to see.

Example of a Cryptographic Guessing Game

Let's take a moment to work through how this cryptographic variant would work. We'll use a simple scrambler function, too weak to work in practice, but complex enough that you should get the sense of a function that's hard to "reverse" and for which your best shot is to guess and check.

The scrambler function will be "raise to the 3rd power, mod 17", or:

$$f(x) = x^3 \bmod 17.$$

That is, multiply the input number by itself three times—so for example 5 goes to 5 x 5 x 5—and then find the remainder after dividing the answer by 17.

Alice and Bob play, with Alice thinking of the secret number and Bob trying to guess. But instead of Alice simply keeping a number in her head, she publicly "commits" to the "scrambled version" number, known as its *hash*. That is, she thinks of a number, puts it through f(x) above, and then announces that value. Let's say she picks 9.

---

[20] The reader may see the similarity to "Special Functions" in the previous section. And indeed, they are the same, except that for "Scrambler Functions," there is no "trapdoor," i.e., no secret knowledge that lets you quickly invert it.

(Note that the only possible outputs she can commit to are 0-16 because of the mod 17 operation.)

She uses the formula above to compute f(9) = 15 (see the footnote if you don't understand why[21]) and only announces that value of 15. It is then Bob's turn to guess numbers and run them through the function until he finds one whose answer is 15. So he might grind through the table below:

x	f(x)
0	0
1	1
2	8
3	10
4	13
5	6
6	12
7	3
8	2
9	**15**
10	14
11	5
12	11
13	4
14	7
15	9
16	16

He would stop at x=9, seeing that it got the result 15. (Note that he didn't need Alice around to verify his guesses, since he could determine himself if they were correct.) As you see, there are 17 possible inputs. If we ignore the zero and assume Alice was picking a number at random, then Bob has to check 8 numbers (half of 16), on average, before getting the correct answer for particular announcement by Alice.

_____

[21] Specifically, 9^3 = 9x9x9 = 729. Then 729 divided by 17 is 42 "and change." But 42x17 = 714, meaning that when you divide 729 by 17, the answer is 42 with a remainder of 15. (Note that 729 – 714 = 15.)

That establishes that there are "cheatproof" games where you can be reasonably certain of how much "work" someone put into winning it. If someone solves a guessing game like this where there are N possible values, the person has, in a sense, proven that he or she "invested" $N/2$ guesses. Sometimes the person might have gotten lucky and needed to make fewer guesses before finding the answer, and sometimes the person needed more, but over time it averages out.

But even if you can prove you made "500 guesses worth of work," that still leaves the question of:

How Do People Invest Work in the Bitcoin Ledger?

Recall how we can play the guessing game—and have a resulting proof of work—based on some public number. In Bitcoin, that number is generated based on the ledger. You take the ledger with the biggest proof of work attached to it, add on the new (signed) transactions you've heard about, but haven't been incorporated, and produce a target number, determined uniquely from those inputs.

When you find a winning guess (a number that, when put through the Scrambler, yields the target or a value close enough[22]), you have a proof of work associated with a ledger update (known in the Bitcoin world as a *block*). When other users decide which transaction ledger to regard as definitive, they count all the work proven to be in previous updates, plus the work associated with your proposed update.[23]

---

[22] Strictly speaking, that "target number" is combined with your guess and hashed, with the goal of producing an output that is close enough to zero, but the problems are equivalent.

[23] Note that this means you have an incentive to build off of the "ledger update set" (blockchain) which itself currently has the most work invested in it, as you get to claim that work, plus the work you put into your own update.

Why Do People Invest Work in the Ledger?

In short, it's because of another rule in the protocol: if you find a solution, you may claim 25 new bitcoins for yourself or any addresses of your choice.[24] (That is, they are bitcoins that weren't previously in circulation.) That reward is what has led to "mining," as it is called: use of specialized computers for generating solutions as quickly as possible, intending to profit by the bitcoins earned this way.

One final complication: You might be wondering if the introduction of specialized, "incentivized" miners leads to faster production of solutions. Actually, one more rule in the protocol specifies that the "difficulty factor," as it is called, should increase or decrease (every two weeks) to ensure that solutions are produced about every ten minutes.[25] And it's easy to modify a Scrambler Function to make it harder or easier to solve: just require a match of more or fewer digits. At the beginning, a solution might have only needed to match the last digit, but as solutions are found more quickly, the "update formula" requires more and more digits to match.

Applied Back to Bitcoin

The above discussion should give a general intuition of how Bitcoin works.

So, let's step back and summarize. Here is a simplified version of what goes on in the Bitcoin network:

---

[24] This reward decreases over time per the spec, halving every four years until all 21 million are in circulation. It started out as 50. The winner also gets to claim any transaction fees offered with the new transactions, which aren't necessary, but encourage users to include them in updates as soon as possible.

[25] The reader may note that we keep casually assuming that users will follow the protocol (taking the highest-work ledger as definitive, requiring a certain difficulty threshold, rejecting double-spends and invalid signatures, etc.) without explaining why. The reason users do this is not because of any law, but because failure to do so would isolate them from the rest of the network, just as with any rule-breaking maverick. We elaborate on this dynamic in the section on creeping centralization.

1) Whenever users want to transfer their bitcoins over to someone else, they broadcast a message describing the transfer and sign it with their private key.

2) Whenever a user receives a message indicating a transfer, he or she first checks that the signature is valid, and that the address doesn't spend more than the latest "confirmed" ledger shows it as having. If it checks out, the user keeps the message and propagates it to others.

3) All users wishing to claim the reward for a solution (aka "miners") bundle up all transactions they know of (i.e., new ones plus those in the latest confirmed ledger), and convert it into the "crypto guessing game" problem for that transaction set. They then work on solving that problem.

4) When someone finds a solution, he or she broadcasts it, with the bundle of known transactions (new latest ledger), to all other users. Like with individual transactions, anyone who receives one of these checks it, and if valid, broadcasts it to others.

5) Miners who receive a new valid solution quit their current search for a solution, then take the latest ledger as definitive. Again, as in 3), they bundle up new transactions they hear of, add them to this new ledger, and try to solve a new math problem unique to the new transaction set, and the process begins anew.

Security Review

Because it may not be obvious, let us go over the security implications of this setup.

Note that users have a unique ledger to go with, as only one of the various ledgers they see at any moment will have the most work invested in it. Those who solve a block (i.e., find the solution for a latest ledger) have every incentive to spread the news, as it ensures the rest of the network will accept and build off of their solution, validating their reward. Occasionally, different parts of the network see different ledger update solutions, each of which becomes "reigning champion" of that subgroup. The disagreement is resolved when someone builds a ledger off of one of those two (or another ledger off of *that*, etc.) until one is several updates ahead of the last, making it unlikely it could ever "leapfrog" into the lead.[26]

But what happens if rogues or thieves try to disrupt this placid setup? As discussed in the previous section, it is technically (nearly) impossible for any malicious user to forge signatures. But let's instead assume they just want to shut down the network by looking for solutions to "empty ledger updates"—that is, they try to make it so that no one can transfer bitcoins. While other miners would include transactions they see, this rogue group would act like no one had been transferring bitcoins the whole time—the equivalent of saying, "Nope, nothing to report here," for the crypto-currency economy. To be sure, honest miners would continue to publish solutions with the transfers, but attackers—if they had enough computational power—would be able to continually "outrun" the rest of the network, publishing a ledger (that happens to be empty) with more proven work invested in it.

Alternatively, imagine that they find solutions as legitimate miners would do, but proceed to publish contradictory updates: say, the update shown to one half the network sees them give the same 50 bitcoins to one address, while the other half sees it given to another; this is what we mean by "double-spending" bitcoins. If this were to occur, one ledger chain eventually would win out, and the other side would have to take the loss as everyone else in the network decided that they weren't the recipients of those 50 bitcoins, after all.

Concretely, the scenario might work like this: Malicious Mallory signs a transfer of 5 bitcoins from an address to Charlie, then signs those same bitcoins away to Diane.

---

[26] The technical term for a ledger update left behind this way is "orphan block." To avoid relying on (what will become) an orphan block, it's recommended that users wait until the first ledger with it is "extended" 5 times.

Mallory finds one solution (call it A) for the first transfer, and another solution (call it B) for the second. Naturally, they can't both happen. Mallory then broadcasts solution A to the section of the network with Charlie, and solution B to the one with Diane. Mallory (quickly) takes possession of the hammers she bought from Charlie with those bitcoins, and the nails she just bought from Diane. However, the next published solution builds off of the one with the transfer to Charlie, and eventually the transfer to Diane is ignored, leaving Diane holding the bag; she traded her nails for nothing.[27]

What would it take to attack the network this way? In order to consistently produce solutions that "beat out" the rest of the network in computational investment, the (cooperating) attackers would need more "hashing power" than the rest of the network combined.[28] This fact ensures that, the more "honest" nodes—meaning those simply including transactions they see into their ledger updates, rather than trying to reject every transaction message or double-spend—that there are in the network, the harder it is to successfully attack the network.

Though it may seem wasteful to keep computing all these hashes, they actually perform an important function, which is to get everyone to coordinate on an unforgeable transaction record, while not having to trust anyone—so long as dishonest nodes do not themselves dominate the network.

---

[27] This is the same basic mechanism as involved in bouncing a check before the merchants can compare notes.

[28] Note that we said "consistently." In reality the 50% threshold for an "attack" on the Bitcoin protocol overstates the requirements for it to work; if a collection of rogues had 40% of the total hashing power of the system, they would be able to frequently double-spend bitcoins. The difference is that with 50% and above, the attackers would be more likely than not to succeed in an individual attempt. Note that even in this situation, sellers could still protect themselves by waiting for additional confirmations (ledger updates with a given transaction) before parting with their goods.

December 2014

IV. How Bitcoin Works: Moving Beyond the Protocol

The previous chapter described how the core Bitcoin protocol works. This chapter reviews the systems and mechanisms that have developed around Bitcoin and have become vital to the crypto-currency "ecosystem" even while not being part of the original specification.

a) Mining pools: dealing with a massive network

As discussed previously, the mining system rewards users in proportion to how fast they can calculate "hashes." The faster they can generate such calculations, the more frequently they will discover a winning "proof of work" at the current difficulty, and the more bitcoins they will mine.

However, the network "hashing power" soon got very large, which similarly raised the difficulty factor. It got to the point where the typical small users could expect, on average, to wait months or even years before they found their first solution and earned their first reward. That wouldn't itself be an insurmountable problem, but keep in mind, the difficulty could increase *during* that time as well—and it could increase so fast as to make that miner uncompetitive before the time of their expected reward, meaning that they were mining for nothing.

Solution: Pooling Miners Together

So, Bitcoin users early on realized they could combine their efforts into a more powerful guesser. To the network, they would appear as one user who found solutions more frequently. Their expected per-hash rate of return would not change, but they would receive a steadier payout. Every time the pool finds a solution, they distribute the reward to members, in proportion to how many guesses a member contributed.

To put it in terms of the guessing game, imagine some players working together while agreeing to share the winnings if anyone guesses correctly, thereby increasing their probability of winning. In this respect, we can view joining mining pools as a form of hedging (or insurance), where a bunch of small miners turn their low-probability-of-a-big-reward into a high-probability-of-a-small-reward. To repeat, viewed as a collective group, a pool of, say, 1,000 miners doesn't expect to earn (significantly) more bitcoins over the course of a year than the 1,000 miners individually would earn during that same year, working in isolation.[29] The problem is that any individual's stream of bitcoin earnings would be very sporadic if he or she worked in isolation, perhaps earning nothing for months at a time and then "hitting the jackpot" when finally solving a block and getting the full reward of 25 bitcoins (as of this writing). By "pooling" their mining efforts into one collective team, the 1,000 small miners could make their individual earning stream much more predictable (but smaller of course) week to week. During the course of a year, each miner might expect to earn roughly the same amount of bitcoins whether working individually or as part of the team, but most people prefer a certain stream of income rather than a sporadic one with the same expected payout; economists call this "risk aversion." This is the main rationale for forming mining pools.

Keeping the Members of a Mining Pool Honest

You may be wondering, as we did, how a mining pool knows how much to reward each user. After all, the vast majority of contributors will never find a winning solution, even though they all help to increase the number of guesses the pool can make. So you might have this image of dishonest miners taking advantage of a pool by saying "Well, sure, we tried that block of numbers, but -- gosh, darn it! -- we never found a solution. Well, you win some, you lose some, right? Oh, and don't forget to credit us for trying those possibilities when you guys do find one!"

---

[29] In the chapter below dealing with objections, we return to the issue of "economies of scale" in mining pools.

However, mining pools actually have an ingenious solution to this, which is basically a rework of the very proof-of-work protocol that the actual Bitcoin protocol uses! Just as Bitcoin users can verify how much work someone spent on a problem, so can a mining pool verify how much work its members contributed to a solution.

To get some intuition about how this process might work, think back to the cryptographic guessing game: you declare a target output number, and the guessers have to find an input number that, when put through the scrambler function, results in the target number. For simplicity, let's say there are 1,000 possible outputs, such that you have to guess a thousand possibilities to be sure of a solution, and find one, on average, after 500 guesses. In this example, suppose the miners who have joined the pool know that they are trying to "hit" the target number of 747. So everyone in the pool knows the mathematical function by which an input number is transformed into an output number, and the goal is to find the magic input number that—when plugged into the function—spits out "747" as the answer. Remember, these are one-way functions, meaning it's easy to turn an input into the associated output number, but virtually impossible to go the other way. So that's why they can't just reverse engineer and "solve" directly by going from 747 backwards. Instead, they need to use brute force trial-and-error to keep sampling numbers from the range of 1, 2, 3, ..., 999, 1000 until somebody gets lucky and finds the number that "maps" onto 747 when it is plugged into the function.

Now when the miners join the pool, obviously they will be assigned different subsets of the possible numbers, to ensure that *somebody* in the pool tries the correct number as soon as possible. If there are ten miners in the pool, then the first one might be given the task of trying the numbers 1 – 100, the second person is assigned 101 – 200, and so on, with the tenth member of the pool being assigned 901 – 1,000. Now remember, even though everybody knows that the goal is to "land" on 747, nobody has any idea which *input* number will get there. The scrambler function is so inscrutable that nobody even knows which input numbers will end up *close* to 747, because there is no predictable pattern in how a given input number maps onto an output number. For example, if Jake is the second person in the mining pool, he starts grinding through 101, 102, and 103, and he finds outputs of 851, 282, and 360, respectively. Before running the numbers, neither Jake nor anybody else had any idea that 101 would map onto 851, and even after running through his first three assigned input numbers, Jake still has nothing better to try except to keep plowing through his list and hope that he just gets lucky. It's not as if he can "learn more about the scrambler function" with each guess.

Now as it turns out, in our hypothetical scenario as Jake lets his machine start slogging through the computations of running 104 through the scrambler function, another member of the group—let's say her name is Alice—announces that she's found the solution! Alice was the tenth member of the pool, and she had run through 901, 902, and 903 with no success. But when she fed 904 into her computer and had it run through the computations, the output came out of 747—the target number. So the group as a whole can stop working, and the ten members each split the 25 bitcoins that they were awarded by the Bitcoin protocol.

Now recall the problem that the mining pool faces: how do they know Jake really contributed 100 guesses ("hashes") without having to re-check the results he sent in, defeating the purpose of the pool?

Well, remember that the results of the hashing scatter evenly, even when the inputs are confined to specific groups. Thus, we can figure out the number n of a block of numbers where, no matter how we select those n numbers, 10% of them will map to within a desired range of the target number, so long as we allow "wraparound" where 999 counts as "two away" from 1 and so on. (Remember, in this example there are 1,000 possible output values so 10% of guesses will fall in the 100-199 range, 10% in the 200-299 range, etc.)

Therefore, the only communication the members need to do to with the organizer is to report these "near hits". For example, the people running our hypothetical pool could tell the members to report any instance where they land within ±10 units from the target number of 747. In other words, not only would a member of the pool announce "bingo!" when hitting 747, but he or she would *also* report anytime finding a number that mapped onto any number in the range of 737 through 757. For example, if Jake tries 104 and it maps onto 751, then he would report "104" to the management of the pool, even though it wasn't a winner. They could check to see that yes indeed, 104 *did* map to within 10 units of the target number.

Remember, the whole point of reporting these "near hits" is to be sure that every member of the pool is actually contributing to the team effort by plowing through numbers. The more "near hits" Jake is able to report, the more searching he must have performed; there's no way Jake can know beforehand how to tailor his searches to get near 747. The number of such near hits will be directly proportional to the number of guesses they make, so it will neatly indicate each member's relative contribution, for deciding how big a share of the solution prize to give them. For example, by the time someone on the team actually finds the solution—the number that maps onto 747—suppose Jake has reported 8 near hits while another team member, Charley, only reported 2. Jake would then get a cut off the 25 bitcoins that was four times greater than Charley, because presumably Jake's computer checked four times as many numbers as Charley's did, during the search time.

To be clear, for our example we just arbitrarily assumed that the ±10 units from the target, a "near hit" range that works out to 1% of the original domain. There is a tradeoff here to tweaking that threshold of "nearness": The wider the net, the more accurate the payment distribution will be, with the members of the mining pool being rewarded more closely to the actual contribution they made. The downside though is that the people running the pool have to *verify* the near hits, to be sure that the members aren't simply lying. This itself takes precious computational power, with the management running through calculations that won't lead to any bitcoins.

In the abstract, it's not obvious what the optimal point is on this spectrum, especially when with members who have vastly different computational powers and where some members of the pool could be unscrupulous. On the one end of the spectrum, there could be an extremely tight window of "nearness," where members of the pool only announce the actual winning solution—a range of ±0, if you will. This would have no "drag" on the computational power of the pool, because there would be no checking necessary, but then it would mean that all the members split the 25 bitcoins evenly, because there would be no way to know how many guesses each member had attempted before one of them found the winner.

On the other end of the extreme, the management could insist that participants in the pool report a near hit within ±499 of the target. But that would simply lead them to report *every* guess. After the fact, if management went through and verified the guesses submitted by each member of the pool, then they would be *certain* of the relative contributions of each member (since management would have double-checked every single guess claimed by every member). But obviously, that would defeat the purpose of the pool, if management had to devote its own computers to duplicating all of the calculations that its members had performed.

We have devoted so much time to this discussion for two reasons: First, it helps shed light on the broader operation of Bitcoin itself, which is the main purpose of this guide. Second, one of the most clever objections to Bitcoin concerns "economies of scale" in mining pools. Later on, we will try to address this objection, but our task then will be much easier now that we've methodically explained the basics of mining pools.

Stealing the Solution?

Another worry for people joining a mining pool might be the reverse: that one of the members could find the solution, and instead of passing it back to the pool owner for sharing, they could run off with it and claim it all for themselves. Fortunately, pools have a (cryptographically secure) way of preventing this as well: members find a solution (or "nonce") for a hash of a transaction bundle, but not the content of that transaction bundle itself. So they don't have the necessary information to redeem solutions they find.

The pool leader *could*, however, refuse to pay out after finding a win, so to this extent they depend on reputation for properly allocating the reward. Fortunately, the members can verify that a) the rate they're earning credits (near hits) matches their rate of guessing, and b) their share of the reward makes sense given the number of credits they contributed and number of "near hits" needed to find a solution.

b) Bitcoin exchanges

Just as there are sites like eBay for coordinating buyers and sellers, and foreign exchanges for coordinating those who convert between currencies, there are sites that facilitate exchanges between bitcoins and conventional currencies. In a typical Bitcoin exchange, the exchange owner will take "physical" possession of both the Bitcoins and conventional monies (from the perspective of the Bitcoin network, an address held by the owner is also the owner of the bitcoins).

When bitcoins are traded within such an exchange, it is unlike the usual in-network bitcoin transfers. No signed message is produced and broadcast, and the transfer doesn't have to show up in any ledger update; it's an internal accounting matter for the exchange. Only when the time comes to move the bitcoins out of the exchange, to honor the promise, do they need to follow the usual Bitcoin protocol.

For an analogy with paper currency, imagine Alice deposits $100 in physical cash into her checking account with CitiBank. CitiBank takes physical possession of the green pieces of paper, and in its own bookkeeping says that Alice has an additional $100 in her account. Alice can check this number online or by consulting an ATM. Then if Alice writes a check to Billy, who is also a CitiBank client, there is no physical movement of currency. No, CitiBank still keeps the currency in its vaults, but merely changes its records by subtracting $100 from Alice's account and adding $100 to Billy's. Of course, if Billy wants to *withdraw* money from his CitiBank account, then the bank must give up physical possession as it simultaneously subtracts the amount from Billy's account.

The same process occurs with Bitcoin exchanges. When Alice deposits a bitcoin with the exchange, it "takes possession" in the sense that she formally transfers control over the bitcoin to an address controlled by the exchange; the Bitcoin public ledger now views the exchange as the owner of that bitcoin, with the authority to decide whether it will be spent (transferred to someone else) in the future. Now when Alice does this, the exchange (if it is honest) will use internal bookkeeping to reflect the fact that Alice has deposited one bitcoin with it. If she tells the exchange to transfer the bitcoin to Billy (perhaps because he sold her a desk), the exchange can retain control of the bitcoin vis-à-vis the Bitcoin ledger so long as Billy himself is a client of the exchange; it merely subtracts 1 BTC from Alice's balance and adds it to Billy's. But if anyone wants to withdraw bitcoins out of the exchange, then it must transfer control of them by sending the appropriate instructions to the Bitcoin network, so that the ledger can be updated accordingly.

c) Payment processors

Whatever the merits of the Bitcoin network, it must exist within a world in which not everyone accepts it or works in it. But if its promoters wish to increase its acceptance rate, it will be important for people to be able to spend it in more and more places. The role of payment processors is to do a transparent conversion between Bitcoin and conventional currencies so that the customer spends bitcoins while the merchant perceives that he is being paid in a more traditional currency (such as the dollar or euro). Specifically, what happens here is that behind the scenes, the payment processor takes in the bitcoins from the customer, while simultaneously issuing the desired currency to the merchant, according to the prevailing exchange rate at the time of sale (with a built-in margin so that the processor can earn a fee on the deal). The payment processor has access to a market (perhaps a large Bitcoin exchange) where it can sell bitcoins for the target currency as needed, in order to maintain its holdings of various currencies to allow speedy transactions.

The service might sound elaborate, but it is similar to what many credit card companies do when their clients travel abroad and use their credit card to buy items denominated in foreign currencies. The buyer and seller both see a transaction in their own currency (often with a fee), based on the market exchange rate at the time of the sale, while the issuer silently converts without further effort on either's part.

d) Mixing pools

While Bitcoin allows for the potential of anonymity, it requires a certain amount of work to reap such benefits. All transactions are public, so anonymity requires constantly generating new addresses to which to steer incoming payments, so that there is no unique connection to its original holder. This requires coordination between users to send their coins to random new addresses that obscure their origins. If you simply used the same address for every transaction, then your entire history would be visible as soon as someone can tie you to any one of them—perhaps by selling something to you and asking that you send bitcoins as payment.[30]

---

[30] Merchants are advised for this reason to generate a unique address for each transaction:

As noted before, users can create many addresses on their own (as many as they like), and shift their money around at will, but it adds a significant additional layer of privacy to ensure that their transactions don't simply lead directly to the same person that created these addresses. In a mixing pool, a user partners with others so that the original bitcoins are spread not just among many addresses, but among many users. The money would end up in new addresses as above, but most of it would have "come from" other users. For example, instead of paying out to 5 addresses, the user might pay out to 95 addresses, while receiving money in 5 addresses that "really" came from other people.

That way, even if a motivated investigator did find a transaction path connecting a known transfer back to the person under investigation, it would be of limited evidential value; that person would be one of many people that the bitcoins passed through. An analogy can be drawn here to the use of cash. According to a study, 90% of dollar currency notes in the U.S. have trace amounts of cocaine on them.[31] Yet for that very same reason, the possession of such cash is weak evidence, or inadmissible as such, precisely because everyone, not just drug users and dealers, is carrying such notes. Mixing pools accomplish something similar: they make it so that one person's bitcoins are well-mixed into other addresses, creating a situation where a target of an investigation could honestly say, "Yes, there is a chain of transactions connecting one of my known addresses and that one you cite...but you could say that for 90% of the network!"

---

https://en.bitcoin.it/w/index.php?title=Merchant_Howto&oldid=52425#Common_Errors

[31] See:
http://www.acs.org/content/acs/en/pressroom/newsreleases/2009/august/new-study-up-to-90-percent-of-us-paper-money-contains-traces-of-cocaine.html

e) Embedded messages

The protocol allows for arbitrary messages, unrelated to Bitcoin transactions, to be attached to a transaction. While this may seem like a needless distraction, it actually inherits all the timestamp properties of the transfers in the actual blockchain, which itself establishes an un-forgeable, chronological event record. That is, it provides validation that the entire network has seen the message within a small window, effectively timestamping it. In fact, a developer wrote a tool that "piggybacks" off the existing Bitcoin network to embed messages.[32] And a variant of the Bitcoin protocol (Namecoin) is already used as a way of recording transfers of Internet domain names in a way that's more resistant to fraud than conventional ways of authenticating people;[33] the same basic idea could be extended to other property.

f) Scripting and smart contracts

The protocol allows for a limited amount of automation, so that you can "trigger" certain events to happen later, conditional on approval from later parties. A common example would be escrow services: normally, you need a third party to hold on to money until the parties agree on who gets to keep all of it. But with scripting, you can make the network adhere to the rule that "in two weeks, the funds go to either party A or B, as determined by party C," without having to enable any one party to have physical possession, avoiding the risk of someone running off with the money.

---

[32] See: http://news.techworld.com/security/3449015/could-the-bitcoin-network-be-used-as-an-ultrasecure-notary-service/
[33] See: http://namecoin.info/

V. The Promise of Bitcoin

In Chapter II we explained the problems with State-issued currencies. Because Bitcoin is a private currency, widespread adoption of it would mitigate all of the evils of the State's monopoly on money. First and foremost, the menace of *inflation* would be forever vanquished—households and businesses could make long-term plans with much more confidence about the market value of the currency.

In this respect, note that Bitcoin is superior to even the traditional commodity monies of gold and silver. The precious metals are obviously much more stable in their growth rate than State-issued fiat currencies, but they too can "inflate," and with less predictability than Bitcoin with its internal feedback mechanism by which the difficulty of mining is periodically adjusted. Although it's a bit fanciful, we note that even "hyperinflation" is possible with gold and silver, if (say) humans discover a massive new deposit (perhaps in an asteroid belt) or if scientists one day can figure out how to cheaply manufacture gold and silver out of other elements in the lab.

In contrast, Bitcoin is the *ultimate* in "hard" money, even though it's intangible. Its scarcity is not due to empirical likelihood (as is true for gold and any other commodity money), but is mathematically embedded in its very protocol. By design, Bitcoin will be forever capped at (just under) 21 million units.

There is another important advantage that Bitcoin possesses over traditional commodity monies. To appreciate this advantage, we have to first explain a simplification that we've been using thus far in the guide. Strictly speaking, widespread adoption of Bitcoin would mean that inflation of the *base money stock* would fall to zero, once the 21 million bitcoins had all been mined and awarded. Yet even in this scenario, if commercial banks accepted deposits of bitcoins and gave customers checking accounts that were only backed up by fractional reserves, then the commercial banks (by making and calling in loans) could expand and contract the broader quantity of "bitcoins in the economy" as measured by everyone's checking account balances. This is analogous to today's situation where (say) the amount of "U.S. dollars held by the public" is larger than the amount of paper currency in existence, because $10,000 in paper currency in the vault of a commercial bank might "back up" $100,000 in total customer checking account balances, as represented by digits in the bank's computer.

So we see that even a hard *base* money doesn't necessarily translate into a stable money, as held by the public, if the commercial banking system operates on a "fractional reserve" basis and (for whatever reason) the banks periodically engage in wide swings in the amount of loans they pyramid on top of their customer deposits of base money. Yet here is where another advantage of Bitcoin comes into operation. Because Bitcoin is both a currency *and* a payment system, a society that used Bitcoin as its money would be much less dependent on large banking institutions.[34] Maintaining a "Bitcoin wallet" is, practically speaking, the same thing as opening an online checking account (with 100% reserves). Note that as more and more merchants and employees began to accept Bitcoin, the need for "Bitcoin exchanges" would also diminish. To be sure, there would still be commercial banks and other "middlemen" institutions even in a world that used only Bitcoin as its money, but the power of banks to inflate the currency would be greatly curtailed, even compared to a world where everyone used gold as money.

Beyond stability in the value of money, the elimination of monetary inflation would also eradicate the business cycle as we know it, as credit markets could no longer be whipsawed by the whims of central bankers. Furthermore, by taking the power of the printing press away from the politicians, States would have to finance their wars and welfare programs through explicit taxation or borrowing from private lenders.

---

[34] Indeed, one of the primary motivations of Satoshi Nakamoto to develop Bitcoin was to eliminate the fees that "middlemen" organizations could charge for the transfer of funds.

This would reveal the true burden of these expenditures, thereby ushering in a more productive and peaceful world.

We should also mention that the widespread adoption of Bitcoin would greatly enhance financial privacy for the average citizen. Make no mistake, if the government targets a particular individual on its hit list, Bitcoin will not protect him. State investigators with a large budget and plenty of free time can eventually find a weak link and tie a Bitcoin address to a real person in the target's human network, and begin to unravel the Bitcoin transactions.

However, just because Bitcoin won't allow (say) members of ISIS to operate with complete invisibility, it nonetheless will make it *much* easier for an average person to shield his financial activities. This will allow him to (say) make donations to unpopular targets like Wikileaks, because Bitcoin doesn't have centralized "choke points" the way some other digital payment systems do, like credit cards, PayPal, or e-gold.

The advantages of Bitcoin are most obvious when it comes to underdeveloped regions of the world that are not served by sophisticated financial institutions. Entrepreneurs in Africa can much more easily connect with venture capitalists in Europe if the world moves toward Bitcoin. Furthermore, it would be quite difficult for governments to prevent "repatriation of profits" when all that the local business owner needs is an Internet connection to transfer some of the earnings back to the foreign investors.

As a final consideration in our brief description of the promise of Bitcoin, consider how it can revolutionize escrow services. Financial transactions traditionally involved the danger of someone running away with the money, inviting heavy government scrutiny and requirements for record-keeping. Even today, when most money isn't physical, there is the danger of a fiduciary using his access rights to embezzle the money. This has led governments to impose strong requirements before one can act as an escrow, usually mandating disclosure of personal information and putting significant funds in a trust. This, in turn, makes it harder to find someone who can conduct an escrow arrangement.

Under the Bitcoin protocol, transactions can be encoded so that it's *impossible* for the escrow provider to violate the trust: the "smart contracts," encoded in the protocol's scripting language, make it so that the bitcoins only go to specific parties based on known conditions. Therefore, people only need to a) trust the escrow to make the right decision in a dispute, and b) have a "fallback" condition in case there's no decision from the escrow agent.

Note the lower threshold: now, anyone can provide the service without having to make a PayPal-scale financial network or get the certifications and capitalization currently required because you don't need to actually hand anyone the money.

VI. Common Objections to Bitcoin

➔ *"The Bitcoin network is enormously wasteful in terms of energy."*

Critics often point out the enormous energy spent on server farms to mine bitcoins, and the extensive "arms race" as miners have to commit ever-greater resources to produce the same coins.

However, the dynamics are not significantly different from those of actual gold mines, in which more resources must be spent to dig up the next unit of gold, as the easier finds are exhausted. Indeed, Bitcoin's Keynesian critics recognize as much when comparing Bitcoin to gold.[35]

The "competition" between miners to find solutions the fastest, far from being pure waste, is an artifact of it being a trustless protocol, in which the fact of having found a solution *must* convey that a significant portion of the overall computing power of the network was spent on it. This requires, in turn, that greater total investment in faster hash computations will be followed by a larger number of hashes per mined bitcoin, no different from how gold tends to require a greater investment per ounce to mine over time.

The Bitcoin network is far from alone in being a situation where lack of trust necessitates spending. For example, we might all be better off if we quit stealing from our neighbors altogether, because then we wouldn't have to install locks and security systems. But so long as we don't live in a world where people are meticulously honest, then resources spent to secure these boundaries are not wasted. And as long as States will take advantage of their control of money, it is not

---

[35] See in particular Paul Krugman's 2013 article "Bits and Barbarism," although he makes the comparison unfavorable to Bitcoin.

a waste to use a system that requires a computational proof of work instead of trusting a single party to determine the transaction ledger.

→ *"How does it improve privacy to disclose every transaction to the world?"*

Bitcoin uses a different "privacy model" from conventional banking. Normally, your connection to an account number is disclosed to counterparties and intermediaries (i.e., the financial institutions that process the transaction and any employees who may need to access the record), and they keep the transaction record on a "need to know" basis. Bitcoin reverses this: the transaction record is public, while your connection to an account is (optionally) kept private.[36]

Both models have their advantages, but it's important to understand what Bitcoin offers here. With Bitcoin, it's possible to hide the "meaning" of a transaction (to the extent that it's connected to people's identities) from everyone except the two parties to it. In contrast, conventional banking requires that these third parties be able to look up the real owner of an account and "connect the dots" regarding who transferred what to whom. Even respectable, privacy-conscious banks, who keep this information on a need-to-know basis (such as by making it so that the typical employee only sees account numbers without names), must trust others with the information.

Note, however, that, it does require additional effort to keep one's connection to a Bitcoin address hidden. Simply using Bitcoin will allow any recipient of your transfers to see what other addresses have been associated with the one that sent them the money. But for those willing to take the additional steps involved in mixing pools (see previous section), it can buy additional privacy.

---

[36] Nakamoto's original 2008 Bitcoin white paper explicitly contrasts the two models in its section 10.

➜ *The extent of decentralization: "You're telling me the coders can change how it works, but won't later decide to make it inflationary?"*

The Bitcoin protocol and codebase must balance competing concerns. On the one hand, its major selling point is that the rules are "fixed in code," such that an ambitious "central banker wannabe" can't later tweak things because of a trendy new economic theory that somehow justifies inflating away everyone's wealth. On the other hand, bugs and oversights are inevitable, as anyone managing a large software project knows, and it is necessary to make occasional updates in anticipation of these occurrences.

A Review: Private Standards

Bitcoin can be thought of as a "private standard," much like the rules of basketball or the rules of English grammar. They carry no force of law, but remain consistent and stable by virtue of the fact that people must adhere to them in order to get the benefits of interacting with the larger network of users. What stops people from, say, making major changes to their usage of English, is the fact that this "breaks compatibility" with the rest of the English speaking community. Generally, they will suffer from all of the problems of miscommunication with the rest of the world ("wait, you've swapped the meanings of 'cat' and 'dog'?"), while having their changes ignored.

For similar reasons, even the supposed "authorities" in these domains (dictionary editors, authors of books on English grammar, sports referees, etc.) are limited to codifying what is already in common practice, and don't try to make major changes to the standard on their own—at least not without getting significant input from the user base. Generally, the larger the change, the greater the risk of the user base simply rejecting it in practice. Even though you might initially think that a word means "whatever the dictionary says," that's actually not true. If, for some crazy reason, the latest edition of the Oxford English Dictionary said that "up" meant "moving toward the ground," that wouldn't change the definition. No, people would just say, "The new OED is wrong."

On the other hand, English definitions are not written in stone. The English language *does* evolve over time—just look at the language in a Shakespeare play or the King James Bible. So standards tend to change only when the benefits of the new standard outweigh the "broken compatibility" it may introduce.

Very rarely, what happens is a "fork," in which different subsets of the community recognize a different history as being the valid one—perhaps England and the United States accept different spellings of words, or different sports leagues adhere to different rules (such as allowing a designated hitter in baseball). This can happen in the Bitcoin network as well, which would correspond to the case where the two subsets recognize different owners of the same coins as of some point, leading to increasingly divergent and isolated ledgers.

Case Study: The Accidental Bitcoin Fork of March 11, 2013

It may be illustrative to review a time when a change to the code was urgent. Though the details are complicated technically,[37] what essentially happened was this: a new version of the code was released on March 11th that occasionally counted different transactions as valid compared to a previous version. This created an accidental fork, where different traders thought different ledgers were valid, and thus disagreed on account balances, and which purported solutions to accept or reject, as they would be proofs of work for (what the other branch regarded as) invalid transactions.

---

[37] A full account is available from Bitcoin Magazine at:
http://bitcoinmagazine.com/3668/bitcoin-network-shaken-by-blockchain-fork/

Within hours, core developers became aware of the problem and issued an emergency notice advising users to roll back to the previous version of the code, which (unfortunately for some) had the result of voiding their block rewards on the "losing" branch of the fork, but otherwise reconciled accounts.

However, while not exactly inflation, this may reflect the fears of some hard money proponents regarding Bitcoin: if a few bigwigs could all agree to void someone's holdings, why couldn't they also debase others by issuing more? But note the circumstances that forced this particular solution: the alternative was to cleave the network, making new bitcoins only spendable on one "side" of the fork. And whatever option they wanted to take would have voided the last several hours of one branch's work. Getting everyone to go along with the same solution required there to already be a pre-existing consensus in the community that going with one branch or the other was important, but not both.

Like with dictionaries or official sports rules, this core group of developers was only able to push the community toward one side or another on a single point of disagreement, not change their minds about critical features the crypto-currency should have. To return to the dictionary analogy, people will often hail the entry of a new word—such as *blog*—as definitive proof that it's a "real word," but the only reason a word gets *in* a new edition of a dictionary is that the community has already been using it, and everybody recognizes that the word's inclusion is a judgmental call. If the editors of a respected dictionary put in a truly nonsensical word such as *grungerdut*, or removed a word such as *dog*, then that dictionary would no longer be respected as an authority. English speakers would not suddenly start using *grungerdut* nor would they stop using *dog*.

To sum up, although it is theoretically possible, adding inflationary characteristics to the main Bitcoin protocol would be akin to English users in the future deciding they don't want to use verbs anymore, or for chess to have a new piece (the cannon, say) introduced. People who are gradually brought into the Bitcoin network soon come to realize that its cap on the total number of bitcoins is an essential part of the protocol; to deviate from this aspect would make it no longer Bitcoin, in the eyes of the network.

→ *"Bitcoin isn't an actual money, like dollars or euros. People don't think in terms of bitcoins, they still think in terms of those government currencies."*

This objection is probably true for most users of Bitcoin as of this writing (in late 2014). Even people who are willing to accept Bitcoin in trades will often base the number of bitcoins on their prevailing exchange rate with some other currency (such as the USD) at the time of the transaction.

However, this observation by itself doesn't really prove much. If Bitcoin (or some superior crypto-currency that has yet to emerge) ever *did* become a viable alternative to the fiat currencies of the world, it would necessarily occur gradually, as the network of acceptance grew. Before we could witness a large network of people using Bitcoin as their genuine money, we would first see a small but growing network of people using Bitcoin as a *medium of exchange*.

The term "medium of exchange" is used by economists to mean a good that is accepted in a trade, even though the recipient has no *direct* use for the good. Rather, the person accepts the medium of exchange with the intention of buying something else with it, down the road. Thus the good is a "go between" the original act of selling and the subsequent act of buying; these ultimate transactions go "through" the medium of exchange, just as sound waves go through the medium of air, or a telephone line is a medium of communication, relaying a message from one person to another.

There is no question that Bitcoin *is already* a medium of exchange. In other words, right now, as you are reading these words, there are people on Earth selling valuable goods and services in exchange for bitcoins. Furthermore, these sellers are doing so *not* because they plan on eating the bitcoins, or using them to cut down a tree—obviously. Yet we can say more than that: Many of the people who are currently accepting bitcoins in trades *plan on buying other goods and services with them*, rather than merely holding them for speculative reasons because they think Bitcoin is a "good investment" right now. Whether the analyst thinks these people are clever or stupid, the point is undeniable: They are selling goods in exchange for bitcoins, with the intention of using those bitcoins in the future in order to buy goods from other people. These activities are not "investing in" or "speculating in" Bitcoin, they are rather the *definition* of adopting something as a "medium of exchange" as economists use that term.

Now, what makes something a *money*? (And here we're speaking *economically*, not in terms of legality.) Well, that's a harder hurdle to pass. The way we use these terms,[38] a money is a special kind of medium of exchange, namely one that *just about everyone in the community accepts*. Just as every poodle is a dog, but not every dog is a poodle, we can say that every money is a medium of exchange, but not every medium of exchange is money. The reason economists would say that the dollar, for example, qualifies as the money in the United States is that most Americans are willing to accept U.S. dollars in trade when they are selling something. The process is reinforcing: If 95% of the community starts out accepting dollars in trades, then the remaining 5% will probably come on board too, because they know they will have no trouble obtaining what they ultimately desire, if they enter the marketplace armed with dollars.

---

[38] We are using the terminology and framework for monetary economics developed by Ludwig von Mises, a giant in the school of Austrian economics. We are spending time carefully developing the distinction between a medium of exchange and money because this is crucial to defusing a later objection, regarding Mises' "regression theorem." For the most sophisticated discussion of these issues, Mises' classic work *The Theory of Money and Credit* is available for free online here: http://mises.org/library/theory-money-and-credit. However it is a challenging book and newcomers are encouraged to consult Murphy's accompanying study guide: http://mises.org/library/study-guide-theory-money-and-credit.

With Bitcoin, emerging *de novo* as a new currency with no ties to pre-existing monies and their established networks (the way the euro, say, came in with an official link to the original European currencies such as the franc, mark, etc.), the road to money-hood would obviously be a gradual one. Bitcoin would first start out as a medium of exchange, with a growing network of people willing to accept it. We have seen precisely this process unfold before our very eyes, since the first genuinely economic transactions involving Bitcoin occurred in 2009.[39]

So at what point would Bitcoin ever become a bona fide money? Here it's a little tricky in applying the conventional economic definition, because Bitcoin's ease of payment facilitates transactions around the world. For example, if there are 10,000 Earthlings who would accept Bitcoin *first* as payment, and only settle for other currencies as a fallback option, then it might seem as if we've identified a community where Bitcoin is the money. Yet the problem is that these people could be scattered all over the planet, without being able to interact much with each other.

To avoid this type of ambiguity, we propose a simple test: Something qualifies as *the money* used by a community of people when they can go through their daily lives without having to swap it for other currencies. So if it ever gets to the point where people can earn their income in bitcoins, then pay their groceries, rent, electricity, and transportation in bitcoins, we will clearly be able to say that Bitcoin is the money for that group of people, however large or small it may be.

In this guide, we are not necessarily predicting that Bitcoin will become money in this fashion—especially any time soon—but it's important to clarify our thinking about the issue. We want readers to at least understand *what it would mean* for

---

[39] For an excellent discussion of the history of Bitcoin, especially as it relates to issues of monetary economics—though we do not necessarily endorse all of the author's conclusions—see Peter Šurda's (2014) "The origin, classification, and utility of Bitcoin." A brief history of Bitcoin transactions is also available at: https://en.bitcoin.it/wiki/History.

Bitcoin to move beyond a medium of exchange and become a genuine money, in terms of individuals' economic behavior rather than official government edicts.

→ *"Bitcoin is just a giant bubble, or Ponzi scheme! The only reason someone would accept it, is that he thinks he can pass it off on the next sucker."*

The irony of this objection is that it is true for *any* money (or medium of exchange, for that matter). Forget Bitcoin for a moment, and think about standard government fiat currencies. For example, why would a teenager be willing to cut his neighbor's lawn for $20? It's because he has a rough idea of what he'll be able to buy in the marketplace with that $20, and values those items more than the leisure time he sacrifices to cut the lawn. In other words, the "only reason" the teenager accepts the $20 bill as payment from his neighbor is that he expects to pass it off on somebody else.

This pattern holds even for commodity money. For example, in the year 1830 if someone sold a horse for a certain weight of gold, it would almost certainly be because the person planned on buying something else with the gold—rather than (say) turning it into a necklace and wearing it as a new piece of jewelry. Here too, when economists explain gold *as a money*, then people's willingness to accept it in trade is directly driven by their predictions of its purchasing power in the (near) future. In short: People in the 1800s were willing to accept gold as payment, because they were confident they could convince other people in turn to accept the gold as payment.

Now to be sure, a commodity money such as gold has a "floor" on its exchange value, based on its direct uses. In other words, so long as people are still using gold as jewelry or for dental fillings, then a person accepting gold as payment would never have to worry about its market value dropping to literally zero. However, to the extent that plenty of people around the world are currently holding gold for "monetary" reasons, then it is in a "bubble" the way the critics use that term against Bitcoin. The demand to hold gold "as a money" (or medium of exchange, if we want to be purists) pushes up the market price of gold, compared to other items. That means a portion of gold's current market value is due to it being a "Ponzi scheme" in the framework of the Bitcoin critics. In this respect, at best the difference between the "gold bubble" is that it has a floor price above zero, while Bitcoin has a floor of zero. Yet it would hardly be consolation for a gold investor if it lost (say) 90% of its market value soon after he acquired it; he would still regret buying at the peak of a bubble.

We realize these remarks will be quite controversial in certain quarters, particularly among hard-money enthusiasts who are fans of the great Austrian economist Ludwig von Mises. Therefore let us defend our claims above by quoting from Mises himself, writing in 1912 when gold was still the world's money:

> Many of the most eminent economists have taken it for granted that the value of money and of the material of which it is made depends solely on its industrial employment and that the purchasing power of our present day metallic money, for instance, and consequently the possibility of its continued employment as money, would immediately disappear if the properties of the monetary material as a useful metal were done away with by some accident or other. Nowadays this opinion is no longer tenable, not merely because there is a whole series of phenomena which it leaves unaccounted for, but chiefly because it is in any case opposed to the fundamental laws of the theory of economic value. To assert that the value of money is based on the non-monetary employment of its material is to eliminate the real problem altogether.[40]

---

[40] Ludwig von Mises, *The Theory of Money and Credit* ([1912] 1953), pp. 103-104, available for free online here: http://mises.org/library/theory-money-and-credit. For help with this relatively difficult book, see Murphy's accompanying study guide: http://mises.org/library/study-guide-theory-money-and-credit.

To sum up: Yes, the critics are right when they say that the only reason people would accept bitcoins as payment, is that the recipients expect to be able to unload them (at a certain price range) down the road to other people. But that logic holds for *all* monies, including government fiat paper currencies and the historical commodity monies such as gold and silver. As one of the pioneers in monetary theory Ludwig von Mises alludes to in the above quotation, "the real problem" for the economic theorist is to explain the value of money *without* reference to its direct uses.

In short, there is a sense in which Bitcoin has been "in a bubble" since the moment it was first used in an economic exchange. But by the same token, gold has been "in a bubble" for thousands of years, since the first transaction when someone accepted gold because he (or she) planned on trading it away again in the future, and mainstream fiat currencies have been in a bubble since their inceptions. If that's how the Bitcoin critics want to use the term "bubble," so be it, but these are bubbles that can last thousands of years, and which include the very same currencies that the critics themselves use on regular basis.

→ *"Bitcoin isn't a tangible commodity, like gold or silver. It has no intrinsic value."*

There is a lot that the critics (usually) have packed into this type of objection. In the other objections we are handling in this section, we will hit some of the related issues. For right now, however, we can dispose of the "no intrinsic value" claim pretty quickly: *In modern economic theory, there is no such thing as intrinsic value.*

Ever since the so-called Marginal Revolution of the early 1870s, economists rid themselves of the classical way of thinking and embraced *subjective* value theory. This explains market prices in terms of the *mental judgments* that people make when entering the marketplace. In the ultimate analysis, the reason goods have the prices they do, is that the people buying them have *subjective* valuations.

People buy beer because they value it (even though others hate alcohol). People buy cigarettes because they value them (even though others hate them). People buy Bibles because they value them (even though atheists don't). Yes, there are physical characteristics about these various items that help explain *why* people subjectively value them, but the crucial point is that economists explain market prices by reference to *subjective* values; there is no such thing as an object having "intrinsic value." That type of statement literally doesn't mean anything in modern (post-1871) economic theory.

➔ *"Bitcoin can never become money, because that would violate Ludwig von Mises' 'regression theorem.'"*

Most readers can safely skip this objection, since it is so much "inside baseball." However, we have observed that within the libertarian community—a group that would otherwise be very predisposed to consider Bitcoin—this reference to Mises' regression theorem is one of the chief objections.

To explain the (apparent) problem, we have to first give a crash course on Mises' contributions to monetary theory.[41] As we mentioned earlier in this guide, in the early 1870s economists ushered in a new way of explaining market prices, based on *subjective* value and what was called "marginal utility." Ultimately, the reason a pound of steak (say) traded for more than a pound of hamburger meat, was that consumers subjectively valued the steak more than the hamburger. With this

---

[41] A more elaborate explanation is provided in Murphy's article, "The Origins of Money and Its Value," available at: http://mises.org/daily/1333. For a lecture on the same topic—directly tied to the controversy over Bitcoin—see Murphy's presentation at the 2014 Texas Bitcoin Conference, available at: https://www.youtube.com/watch?v=HVnCEWcdEQk.

framework of marginal utility, economists could explain the "real" exchange ratios between commodities, or what we might think of as "barter prices."

Of course, in the real world people don't engage in barter, but instead they (typically) sell everything against units of money, and then use the money for whatever they want to buy. Economists initially thought that it wouldn't work to apply the new, subjective value theory to money itself, because it seemed they would be arguing in a circle. This is because the only reason people value money *in its role as money* (as opposed to the industrial or ornamental uses it might serve, if a commodity money like gold) is that they expect it to have purchasing power in the future. Thus, it seemed as if the cutting edge "marginal utility" approach to explaining economic value didn't really work for the specific commodity serving as a money, because you would ultimately be saying, "People value money because money has value." Framed in this way, such an explanation is hardly convincing; it asserts the very thing economists are supposed to be explaining.

Mises solved this problem with his so-called *regression theorem*. First, he brought in the time element to break out of the alleged circularity. A more precise application of the new, subjective marginal utility theory goes like this: People *today* are willing to accept money in trades, because they expect it will have a certain purchasing power *tomorrow*. Furthermore, people form these expectations about tomorrow's value of money, by the prices of goods (quoted in money) that they observed *yesterday* in the marketplace. Thus, Mises showed that we're not arguing in a circle. Instead, we're ultimately explaining *today's* purchasing power of money—how much stuff a person can buy with a unit of money—by the memory of what money could fetch in the market *yesterday*. The purchasing power, or exchange value, of money today is *not* the same thing as the purchasing power of money yesterday, and so we're not arguing in a circle after all.

Ah, but the critics might not be satisfied with Mises' rhetorical move, so far. Sure, he broke out of the circularity of the explanation, but now it seems he is vulnerable to a charge of an "infinite regress." Mises is ultimately explaining today's value of money by yesterday's value of money. And where, pray tell, did yesterday's value of money come from? Well, from its value *two* days ago, and so on. So it seems that Mises still hasn't solved the problem; he's just pushed it back a step.

This is where Mises really shines, and why so many people to this day revere him as a brilliant economist. Mises pointed out that his explanation did *not* rely on an infinite regress. No, he only had to push back the chain—where the value of money on Day T was influenced by observations of its value on Day $(T-1)$—until the first day that the commodity in question was held by someone as a medium of exchange. Before that fateful transaction, the commodity (let's say it's gold) was a regular good, which was traded in a state of barter and valued purely for its direct uses. Economists already knew how to explain *barter* prices using the new subjective value theory, and so the explanation could stop at that point. Mises had thus incorporated even the money commodity into the new framework of marginal utility theory, showing that his predecessors had thrown in the towel prematurely when they assumed that money itself couldn't be handled with the new mental apparatus.

Now that we've sketched the historical development of monetary theory in the hands of Mises and his Austrian followers,[42] we begin to see the (apparent) problem for Bitcoin: If we use the regression theorem to trace the purchasing power of money today back to the point at which the money commodity was bought and sold in a state of pure barter, then it seems obvious that all monies must have their origin as regular commodities, which are valued for their direct uses and not because they (also) serve as media of exchange. Even government fiat paper currencies fit this pattern, because historically they were all initially phased in with ties to the

---

[42] We acknowledge that this traditional economic description of the origin of money has recently been challenged by anthropologist David Graeber. It lies well outside the scope of this guide to bring up his objections, but interested readers should consult Robert P. Murphy's 2012 article, "Origin of the Specie," available at: http://www.theamericanconservative.com/articles/origin-of-the-specie/.

commodity monies of gold and/or silver. For example, it's true that nowadays the U.S. dollar is a mere green piece of paper, with no direct use. However, historically the U.S. dollar *was* redeemable in gold and/or silver, payable by the U.S. authorities, and thus its purchasing power today can historically be linked to the purchasing power it "inherited" from gold and/or silver when it was legally linked to these precious metals.

So where does all of this leave Bitcoin? In light of Mises' development of the regression theorem, many of his fans have argued that Bitcoin *can't* become a money, since it lacks the historical role as a mere (non-monetary) commodity. Specifically, the (apparent) problem is that nobody would know what the market value of bitcoins were *before* they were valued for their use in exchange. Thus, trying to explain the market value of Bitcoin using the Misesian regression theorem would lead us into a brick wall; we could never go back in time to the point at which people acquired bitcoins in trades solely for their direct uses.

Our answer to this objection is pretty simple: It has been refuted empirically. If the Misesian regression theorem has anything to say about a commodity needing a history as a "regular good," then the roadblock occurs *for any commodity becoming a medium of exchange.* The critical threshold does *not* kick in as a medium of exchange makes the transition to a money. And, since Bitcoin clearly *is* a medium of exchange already, then it should be clear that the regression theorem poses no obstacle to its future development.

This is a subtle point, so let's restate it from a different angle. It is undeniably true that Mises and some of his prominent followers—in particular, economist and libertarian theorist Murray Rothbard—argued in print that any money must have originally been a regular commodity, in order for people to have had a basis for assessing its relative exchange value against other goods. But the logic of their argument applies to any *medium of exchange* (and in fact Mises and Rothbard say so, explicitly, in various passages). In other words, the "problem" of the regression

December 2014

theorem kicks in for even a single person who is going to accept an item in trade with the intention of trading it away in the future. How is that person supposed to know whether he is being ripped off or not, unless he has a sense of the market value of that item already? So if any reader thinks that Mises showed that any *money* must have originated as a regular commodity, then that reader must also think that Mises demonstrated that any *medium of exchange* must have originated as a regular commodity.

Now various thinkers have put forward explanations of how Bitcoin evades the problem. Some have argued Mises was flat-out wrong; others have argued that people *did* value bitcoins directly (for example as components of a global payment system, or as financial assets that might rise in value, or as ideological weapons against the oppressive State); while others have argued that Bitcoin slipped through a loophole in the regression theorem, by having a very low initial exchange value that made the first recipients say, "Why not?" as they traded away a trivial amount of "real" goods for large numbers of bitcoins, even though at that point they technically had no frame of reference for their market value.

However, in our view it's a rhetorical mistake to get into the weeds of explaining *why* Bitcoin was able to evade the apparent roadblock put up by the regression theorem and become a medium of exchange. The crucial fact is, Bitcoin *has* become a medium of exchange, and so clearly the logic of the regression theorem in no way hinders its possible adoption as a full-blown money. People today *do* have a frame of reference for forming expectations of Bitcoin's purchasing power tomorrow—they can look up its purchasing power yesterday. Misesian monetary theory doesn't require that the individuals in the market today possess the historical knowledge of money's ancient exchange value, from the days of barter. No, the only reason Mises needed the link to barter days was to provide a *logically complete* theory. But in the case of Bitcoin, the economists can argue about *how* it got off the ground till they're blue in the face—the brute empirical fact is that Bitcoin *did get off the ground.*

Today, people in the market have several years and counting of market transactions involving Bitcoin.

We have already written a lengthy reply to this particular (and to some readers, no doubt obscure) objection to Bitcoin, but in the interest of convincing the critics and enlightening all readers, let's try one last argument to defuse the "regression theorem" complaint. Even Mises and Rothbard—the champions of "hard" commodity money and undisputed masters of the regression theorem—admit that gold could still be used as a commodity money *even if its direct uses disappeared*. Above, we gave a quotation from Mises to that effect, and now, let's give a similar quotation from Rothbard:

> Demand for a good as a medium of exchange must be predicated on a previously existing array of prices in terms of other goods. A medium of exchange...can arise only out of a commodity previously used directly in a barter situation, and therefore having had an array of prices in terms of other goods. Money must develop out of a commodity with a previously existing purchasing power, such as gold and silver had. It cannot be created out of thin air by any sudden "social compact" or edict of government.
>
> On the other hand, it does not follow from this analysis that if an extant money were to lose its direct uses, it could no longer be used as money. Thus, if gold, after being established as money, were suddenly to lose its value in ornaments or industrial uses, it would not necessarily lose its character as a money. Once a medium of exchange has been established as a money, money prices continue to be set. If on day X gold loses its direct uses, there will still be previously existing money prices that had been established on day X − 1, and these prices form the basis for the marginal utility of gold on day X. Similarly, the money prices thereby determined on day X form the basis for the marginal utility of money on day X + 1. From X on, gold could be demanded for its exchange value alone, and not at all for its direct use. Therefore, while it is absolutely necessary that a money originate as a commodity with direct uses, it is not absolutely necessary that the direct uses continue after the

money has been established.[43]

Although it made the quotation longer than necessary for our point, we included Rothbard's sweeping statements about the need for a commodity to originate with direct uses in order to reassure our critics that we're not hiding anything. Yes, Rothbard definitely thought that any money must have originated as a regular commodity. But as the quotation above makes clear, the onus falls on the transition to *a medium of exchange.*

Furthermore, Rothbard admits that *once a good had established itself with a history of market exchange values*, then that would provide an anchor for the regression theorem to apply *from that point forward.* In Rothbard's own framework, then, we can replace "gold" with "Bitcoin" and say: So long as Bitcoin's purchasing power had been established and observed on day X-1, there would be no problem with individuals valuing Bitcoin *solely* for its exchange value on day X and beyond, even though Bitcoin served no direct uses.

In closing out this lengthy section, we'll leave the critics with one final argument: If you still think that Bitcoin is a "bubble waiting to crash because it has no intrinsic value," then you must admit that Mises and Rothbard made boneheaded mistakes in the quotations above. For both Mises and Rothbard conceded that gold could continue to function as a viable money, even if it somehow were to lose its direct uses. According to your critique of Bitcoin, Mises and Rothbard must be mistaken, because if gold lost its direct uses, it too would then be "in a pure bubble with no intrinsic value," and hence would be liable to crash to zero at any moment. Of course, maybe Mises and Rothbard *were* wrong, but if you think that, you should stop citing their authority in your critique of Bitcoin.

---

[43] Murray Rothbard, *Man, Economy, and State, With Power and Market* (Scholar's Edition, 2nd edition, [1962] 2009), italics removed, p. 275, available at: http://mises.org/document/1082/Man-Economy-and-State-with-Power-and-Market. See also Murphy's study guide at: http://mises.org/library/study-guide-man-economy-and-state.

Bitcoin has already become a medium of exchange. People can form expectations of its future purchasing power, based on observations of its market value in the immediate past. We are not predicting that Bitcoin *will* eventually become a genuine money, rather we are arguing that at this point, the regression theorem of Ludwig von Mises has no bearing on the question at all. Whether Bitcoin becomes a money, or forever remains a medium of exchange, is a purely empirical question to which the regression theorem has no relevance.

→ *"Isn't a deflationary currency bad for the economy?"*

Some skeptics try to turn Bitcoin's ostensible advantage—the absolute ceiling on the number of bitcoins, at 21 million—into a handicap. By its very design, the Bitcoin protocol adjusts the block reward (how many bitcoins one may claim for finding a valid solution) to yield a constantly shrinking "harvest" of new bitcoins over time, such that 99% of all bitcoins that will ever exist, will be in people's possession probably around the year 2030.[44] This eventual standstill in new "production" of bitcoins leads people to call it a "deflationary currency,"[45] and they worry that it

---

[44] For projections of the increase in bitcoins over time, see:
https://en.bitcoin.it/wiki/Controlled_supply.
[45] Calling Bitcoin "deflationary" is a bit of a misnomer, because technically it is always growing in supply. However, unlike other monies (both commodity and paper fiat) that typically grow exponentially over time, the supply of Bitcoin will taper off as it approaches the hard ceiling of 21 million units. Because the output of "real" goods and services will presumably continue growing at a modest percentage rate year after year (i.e. exponentially), and also because the number of people holding bitcoins will presumably continue to grow, this means that over time the bitcoin-*prices* of most goods and services will go down. *This* is why people call it a "deflationary" currency. Note that when the prices of goods and services *measured in bitcoins* continue to fall, it means that Bitcoin is becoming more and more valuable—you need fewer bitcoins to buy a carton of milk or a new car. If, say, the *dollar*-prices of milk and cars continues to go up over the years, then it means the dollar-price *of one bitcoin* would rise very rapidly, because it would add up the two

would stifle economic growth if large numbers of people relied on Bitcoin as their primary form of money.

These fears are baseless, as we can show using both economic theory as well as historical evidence. A baseline result from monetary theory is that in the long run, the quantity of money is irrelevant to "real" economic variables (such as the unemployment rate, or how many hours a person must work at his job to be able to buy a new car or a basket of groceries). For example, if the total quantity of dollars suddenly doubled overnight—so that people who went to bed with $200 in their checking account with wake up with $400, and so on—then *in the long run*, the main effect would simply be to double all wages and prices. Sure, someone who used to make $50,000 would (eventually) make $100,000 once things settled down, but she wouldn't actually be better off—everything at the store would cost twice as much, too.

Most people can recognize fairly quickly that a doubling of the money supply wouldn't really make society richer. But once a person admits *that*, then the opposite holds as well: Suddenly *cutting the money supply in half* won't make society *poorer*, either, at least once everything adjusts to the new situation. Somebody who initially made $50,000 in salary would (eventually) see her paycheck fall to $25,000, but that wouldn't make it harder for her to live—everything at the store would be half as expensive, too.

Now it's true, so far we've been talking about *the long run*—the economist's favorite refuge where nothing messy happens. What about in the short run? For example, if someone has a mortgage on a house, that's a fixed, contractual obligation quoted in dollars. Whether there is price inflation or deflation, that mortgage payment stays the same. So wouldn't these type of frictions cause serious hardship during an adjustment phase, in response to changes in the money supply?

---

effects (namely, the falling bitcoin-price of goods and the rising dollar-price of those same goods).

The answer is yes, and—drumroll please—it's yet another reason that Bitcoin *is so desirable* as a currency. Changes in the quantity of money only lead to short-run disturbances *if they are unexpected*. But changes in the total amount of bitcoins can be predicted decades in advance, with far more precision than fiat currencies or even commodity monies like gold and silver. If, for example, the bitcoin-price of a general basket of consumer goods fell (say) an average of 5 percent per year from 2030 onward, then people in the year 2028 writing long-term contracts quoted in bitcoins would have seen it coming, and adjusted the terms of the contract accordingly.

It is a modern myth that "deflation" (referring to falling prices for consumer goods) is a bad thing that cripples the economy. Part of the public's fear is a confusion of correlation and causation: Historically economic catastrophes often went hand in hand with falling consumer prices, as people panicked and hoarded cash. Yet that doesn't mean that consumer price deflation *causes* economic depression. For example, from January 1926 through January 1928, the official Consumer Price Index (CPI) in the United States *fell* a cumulative 3.4 percent.[46] Did this gentle price deflation lead to a sluggish economy? No, this happened smack-dab in the middle of the so-called "Roaring Twenties," the boom period that *preceded* the Great Depression of the 1930s. To be sure, consumer prices fell much *faster* during the early 1930s than in the mid-1920s, but it was a matter of degree, not kind.

More generally, there were long stretches in U.S. history during the classical gold standard period when consumer prices gently fell year to year, and yet such mild price deflation was consistent with strong economic growth. Indeed, when the production of goods and services rises faster than the quantity of money (such as the amount of gold people hold), other things equal we would *expect* the purchasing power of a unit of money to increase, as it becomes scarcer relative to everything

---

[46] For historical CPI data see:
http://research.stlouisfed.org/fred2/data/CPIAUCNS.txt.

else. There is nothing dangerous or stifling about this development; it's just the normal operation of supply-and-demand at work.[47]

One glib argument to "prove" consumer price deflation is bad runs like this: When people see prices falling, they postpone purchases. Thus business sales fall off, they lay off workers, people panic and become even more reluctant to spend, and so in a downward spiral to oblivion.

Yet that story *can't* be right, at least as a general rule. First of all, we have historical examples (such as the mid-1920s) when consumer prices gently fell amidst a booming economy. And in our own time, try applying that narrative to the computer industry. Wouldn't that logic "prove" that nobody ever buys a new computer, because he can just wait six months and find better options at lower prices? Yet casual observation informs us that despite the perpetual "deflation" in computer hardware, that industry hasn't been hurting.

There is nothing wrong with people holding *money itself* as a financial asset, which gains value (in terms of its purchasing power in the marketplace) over time. It is a perversity of today's fiat currencies that makes people treat them as hot potatoes, where dollars, euros, and yen "burn a hole in your pocket" if you don't spend or invest them as they constantly depreciate compared to goods and services.

In contrast, someone holding bitcoins would not need to "put them to work" in other financial assets; the bitcoins themselves would appreciate (in terms of general purchasing power) over the years. But to avoid confusion, we should clarify once

---

[47] Economists sometimes use the terms "bad deflation" and "good deflation" to distinguish between falling prices that are caused by a financial crash and falling prices that are caused by "real output" to grow faster than the quantity of money. Obviously, our opinion of (price) deflation will differ, depending on which of these scenarios we associate with the term. See George Selgin's 1999 discussion, "A Plea for (Mild) Deflation," available at:
http://www.cato.org/sites/cato.org/files/serials/files/policy-report/1999/5/cpr-21n3.html.

again that the *social function* of Bitcoin is its service as a currency (and low-cost payment system). The fact that individual bitcoins would appreciate in "market value" over time wouldn't make humanity richer. Rather, Bitcoin's "hard" cap on quantity would make its purchasing power much more predictable than that of other possible monies, and therefore would make it correspondingly more suitable in coordinating long-term economic planning.

Before leaving this section, we'll plug one last chink in Bitcoin's armor: Some people worry that the market value of bitcoins would eventually rise so much that the regular person couldn't afford them. In the year 2050, if one bitcoin can buy (say) a new luxury car, then won't only the rich hold bitcoins, defeating the purpose of trying to get widespread adoption?

This objection overlooks the fact that people can own *fractions* of bitcoins. The protocol actually allows the blockchain to divide ownership down to eight decimal places, meaning that the original protocol and related software can handle purchases as small as 0.00000001 BTC. Therefore, rather than imagining the world eventually being saturated with 21 million bitcoins, it's more appropriate to think of humanity ultimately holding 2.1 *quadrillion* units of bitcoin currency. Just as Americans use dollars, but quote cheaper items in terms of cents, so too could merchants quote items with a different unit of measurement (not "bitcoins") to denote fractional amounts of the currency. For example, a merchant might simply write "45 mBTC" on a price tag, to indicate that the item cost 45 milli-bitcoins, or 45 one-thousandths of one bitcoin. This could also be written as "4.5 cBTC," denoting four-and-a-half centi-bitcoins. (Note that this is similar to 1 millimeter being one-thousandth of a meter, and one centimeter being one-hundredth.) Furthermore, with consensus of the userbase, the protocol can be updated without disruption to allow even greater divisibility.[48]

---

[48] See "The extent of decentralization" above for the issues involved in making changes to the protocol.

→ *"Why would anyone invest in productive operations if retail prices kept falling year after year?"*

A more sophisticated objection to Bitcoin's likely trend of price deflation is that it would remove the incentive for investors to pour capital into operations. After all, if retail prices are falling year by year, wouldn't it make more sense to stay "in cash" (i.e. bitcoins) and reap the "real" returns as those bitcoins become more and more valuable over time?

This type of worry overlooks the fact that the market prices *for resources* could adjust to the expected *future* price of the retail goods they will produce, fully reflecting the necessary incentives to attract investors. It's easiest to illustrate this concept with a simple numerical example:

Present & (Expected) Future Prices for Investor Considering Wine Business in January 2015			
Prices in January 2015...		**(Expected) Prices in January 2016...**	
Bunch of grapes	100 mBTC	Bunch of grapes	98 mBTC
Bottle of 1yr Wine	103 mBTC	Bottle of 1yr Wine	101 mBTC

In the table above, we see that there is a general price deflation in our hypothetical economy, when measuring prices in bitcoins. A bunch of grapes (where "bunch" is the amount needed to make a bottle of wine) has a price of 100 mBTC in January 2015, but twelve months later its price will drop down to 98 mBTC, meaning that grapes have experience 2% price deflation. Similarly, the price of a bottle of wine that has been aged one year falls from 103 mBTC in January 2015 down to 101 mBTC a year later, meaning wine has experienced price deflation of about 1.9%.

So does this general price deflation in our hypothetical economy mean that investors would never buy grapes in order to produce and sell future bottles of wine? Not at all. As the table above shows, an investor can spend 100 mBTC in January 2015 to buy the grapes necessary to produce a new bottle of wine. (For simplicity we're ignoring the labor, glass, cork, storage room, and other inputs.) Twelve months later, the bottle contains year-old wine, which at that point can fetch 101 mBTC in the market. Thus our investor enjoys a *nominal* return of 1 percent on his invested capital, and a *real* return of about 3 percent, assuming the bitcoin-prices of most goods and services also fell about 2 percent. In contrast, if the investor had simply sat on the sidelines holding his bitcoins, his nominal return would have been 0 percent, while his real return would have been about 2 percent.

At this point we can bring up an even *more* sophisticated objection, which worries that with a "deflationary" currency, the market-clearing real return could conceivably fall low enough so that the nominal interest rate would hit the "zero lower bound" and prevent the economy from achieving equilibrium. In our simplistic grape/wine example, if the real rate of return (let's suppose) had to be only 1%, rather than the ~3% implied in the table above, then the only way to achieve that would be for the price of wine in 2016 to be *lower* than the price of grapes in 2015. But why would any investor put 100 mBTC into grapes in 2015, in order to produce a bottle of wine that sold for, say, 99 mBTC a year later? It would be better to hold on to the 100 mBTC for a year, which would maintain their nominal value.

These types of discussions usually have in mind the so-called "Fisher relation"[49] (named after economist Irving Fisher) that says:

---

[49] Incidentally, for purists we note that some historians of economic thought will argue that the profession's understanding of "the Fisher relation" bears only a tenuous relation to Fisher's actual writings on the topic. See Robert W. Dimand's 1999 "Irving Fisher and the Fisher Relation: Setting the Record Straight."

Nominal interest rate = Real rate of interest + Expected rate of (price) inflation.

For modern readers who grew up in a world of State-issued fiat currencies, the Fisher relation is most intuitive if we assume *positive* inflation. For example, if investors want a real return of 5% on their money, and prices in general are expected to rise by 2%, then the investors must be paid a nominal (or market) interest rate of 7%—five points to compensate them for postponing their consumption for a year, and an additional two points to adjust for the fact that the money they are being paid back in is weaker than what they originally lent out.

So now, returning to Bitcoin, we can use the Fisher relation to understand the potential problem. Since the nominal interest rate can't go below 0%—because people would do better just to sit on their bitcoins for a year—the worry is that the loan market will hit a brick wall if the expected rate of price *deflation* is higher than the real rate of interest that balances the desires of borrowers and lenders. For example, if consumer prices in general fall (say) 5% per year, then the *lowest* that real interest rates can drop is 5%.[50] But if the real rate of interest that would "clear" the loan market is (say) 3%, then the economy would apparently be saddled with an interest rate that was two points higher than it ought to be. Some economists worry that in this type of scenario, the community in the aggregate would want to save more than it wanted to invest, and that total spending would be insufficient to provide full employment.

The present guide is of course an introduction to Bitcoin, *not* a primer on economic theory.[51] For our purposes, let us make two points in response to worries over this

---

[50] Rearranging the Fisher relation shows us that *Real Interest Rate = Nominal Interest Rate + Price Deflation Rate*. Since the nominal interest rate can't go lower than zero, the real interest rate is always equal to or greater than the price deflation rate.
[51] The truly adventurous (and/or masochistic) can read Robert P. Murphy's 2003 doctoral dissertation, "Unanticipated Intertemporal Change in Theories of Interest," for a full discussion of all of these issues. We note that the framework discussed in

type of scenario: First, with a stable currency (such as Bitcoin once it reaches 21 million units), under normal circumstances we would expect the real rate of interest to more than offset the price deflation rate. Other things equal, the rate of price deflation itself would simply reflect the growth in output. Intuitively, with a stable amount of 21 million bitcoins in the hands of the public, an average growth of (say) 3% in output year after year would make consumer prices (quoted in BTC) fall about 3% year after year. But if people expect their real incomes to grow by 3% per year, then their desire to "smoothen" consumption over time would lead them to demand a comparable premium for postponing their consumption for a year. On top of that, people in general have "time preference," meaning that even if their incomes were stable over time, they would still demand a premium because of a baseline distaste for deferred gratification. Of course in practice, anything's possible, but these considerations show that a deflationary currency (like Bitcoin) shouldn't pose any problem vis-à-vis "high real interest rates" as a general rule.[52]

Second, we note that historically the problems occur (according to the Keynesian economists who think in these terms) when some outside event—like the collapse of an asset bubble—causes a sudden increase in the demand for money (which fuels price deflation), as well as a drop in the market-clearing real rate of interest (as debt-strapped consumers pay down debt and terrified investors just want to hold on to their principal). Yet in our view, these boom-bust cycles are the creature of State intervention into money and banking. A society who used Bitcoin as their primary money would not find themselves in these periodic troughs after a financial crisis. The smooth and steady growth of "the long run" would also exist in the short and medium runs.

---

the text above—in which interest is conceived of as a "real" phenomenon with rates of price inflation tacked on as an adjustment—is not at all how Murphy approaches the subject. But the treatment above is standard in the literature, and it is how Bitcoin enthusiasts are likely to encounter this particular objection.

[52] The serious reader can see a formal treatment of these issues—and the assumptions under which we can be sure that the real interest rate is higher than the growth rate of consumption—in Charles Jones' 2009 discussion posted at: http://web.stanford.edu/~chadj/Consumption2009-11-25.pdf.

December 2014

→ *"Won't government crack down on Bitcoin?"*

As this first edition of the guide is being written, the U.S., Chinese, and other powerful governments are engaging in varying degrees of interference with the adoption of Bitcoin. It is certainly true that these developments will greatly affect *the market value* of bitcoins, and that they even might be the difference between Bitcoin becoming a genuine money, as opposed to a mere financial asset and/or medium of exchange.

However, in our view it is extremely unlikely that even draconian punishments enacted by central governments around the world could literally stop all humans on Earth from using Bitcoin (or a superior derivative). Crypto-currencies are here to stay. For States to stamp out Bitcoin would be akin to States prohibiting alcohol in the face of massive demand for it.

Remember that no one is "in charge" of Bitcoin. So long as just one copy of the blockchain survives on someone's hard drive somewhere on Earth, the Bitcoin network can quickly propagate to thousands of other computers once that person gets online. Even if governments around the world rounded up all current owners of bitcoins and destroyed all knowledge of their private keys, all that would mean is that the bitcoins mined to that point would be forever lost. But nothing would prevent *new* people from joining the network to mine new blocks, and thereby earning the new bitcoins that came "into circulation." From the point of view of the network, the old bitcoins would still "exist," it's just that their owners for some reason (such as, they were executed or they're sitting in prison) never spent them.

To repeat, it is entirely possible that major crackdowns cause the *market price* of bitcoins (quoted in other State-issued currencies) to crash. For this reason, individuals should consider carefully before accumulating a large holding of bitcoins, and businesses should study the regulatory proceedings before investing large amounts in expectation of a new payment system.

December 2014

Yet as far as the question, "Will Bitcoin—or a derivative—be around in 100 years?" we think the answer is an obvious yes. Remember that cocaine has survived massive government crackdowns, and people around the globe still use gold as a hard asset despite the coercive campaign to unseat it as the market's money.

→ *"Doesn't Mt. Gox prove Bitcoin is a scam?"*

For those who are unfamiliar with the history, the Bitcoin ecosystem had its own sort of Bernie Madoff. For a while, the largest exchange for converting between bitcoins and dollars was Mt. Gox (pronounced "mount gawks" and named after a previous business that dealt in cards for the game Magic: the Gathering). Like conventional brokers and exchanges, it required that you hold your money and bitcoins in trust with them, on the promise that you could withdraw them later.

However, it turned out that Mt. Gox fell victim to some cyber attacks and could not honor the debts it made to users (much like an illiquid or insolvent financial institution that lacked proper insurance or lender of last resort). Like Madoff, it instituted ever-longer delays on withdrawals. Soon, a pillar of the Bitcoin ecosystem was failing to do its job, and people lost much or all of what they had entrusted to the exchange. It sent a shockwave through the Bitcoin community.

Mt. Gox is not the same as Bitcoin, nor a necessary part.

While this is a worrisome development, one must be careful to distinguish exactly what failed, and what didn't. Recall that the central innovation of Bitcoin is in allowing people to conduct trades within its network without having to trust any single party, due to a combination of digital signatures and a competitive proof-of-work system. Neither of these was found to have holes. Rather, what failed is an interface with the rest of the world.

A comparison might be made here to State minting systems: their only security goal for their paper notes (like dollars, yen, etc.) is to make them difficult to counterfeit. It would be rather misplaced to blame mints for the time you got mugged, or the time burglars broke into your home, or the time you were tricked into buying a thousand Beanie Babies: so long as you weren't robbed by the ease with which one can produce fake notes, the mints did their job (though other security measures certainly failed in those cases!). Likewise, the goal of the Bitcoin protocol is to similarly prevent the virtual equivalent of counterfeit; by itself, this system does nothing about the traditional problems of unscrupulous scammers or physical intrusion.

If anything, it should reassure us that all of these attacks are on the Bitcoin protocol's links to the world outside of it, and not the protocol itself. This is because all the "weakest links" are outside of Bitcoin proper.

... But caution in new markets is not a bad thing either.

With that said, one should not be too sanguine about what happened. For a while, Mt. Gox was "the" place to convert between bitcoins and dollars. A system is only as strong as its weakest link. No matter what advanced cryptography a financial service provider might use, it's all for naught if the users routinely fail to follow standard security practices, like leaving credentials where others can get to them, or if its site kept accidentally ceding control of users' accounts to hackers. Furthermore, no matter how counterfeit-proof the U.S. dollar is as a paper currency, the people who use dollars on a daily basis must still make sure that their dollars are not stolen through other means, including irresponsible trustees of such assets, or attackers gaining physical access to cash or financial information.

Similarly, no matter how good the Bitcoin protocol is in its core role of providing a secure transaction network, it is vulnerable to the same "old school" attacks as in traditional assets: scammers, irresponsible trustees, and physical access (in this case, to the private keys needed to sign away bitcoins). The reader is advised to use the same caution in dealing with others in Bitcoin as one does in physical cash.

→ *"If mining pools are a 'natural monopoly,' won't that ultimately destroy Bitcoin?"*[53]

A fairly sophisticated objection to Bitcoin runs like this: "Mining pools exhibit 'economies of scale,' meaning that when you double their size, the amount of bitcoins they earn more than doubles. The profit motive then drives all the miners to join together in a giant mining pool, or at least have several large mining pools join forces in a coordinated cartel. But with such computational power controlled by one or a few key individuals, Satoshi Nakamoto's vision of thousands of autonomous miners independently contributing to the integrity of the blockchain becomes a farce. Simple economic law will drive Bitcoin to destroy its own foundation. The dream of a trustless currency and payment system will be shattered upon the cold logic of a monopolistic mining pool."

This objection seems particularly plausible as of this writing, when the mining pool GHash has only pulled back from 50% of the hashing power of the network because of public concern. The whole *appeal* of Bitcoin was that its users wouldn't need to trust the people running GHash or other organizations to do the right thing.

However, this particular worry will likely fade with time as the industry matures. It is true that there are currently (modest) economies of scale in mining pools, because it takes a certain amount of computational "overhead" to package a bundle of transactions and then broadcast it to the miners in the pool to begin processing, and there are also "administrative" tasks that must be handled—such as checking to see

---

[53] We are grateful to helpful discussions with Paul Snow for the material in this section, though any errors remain those of the authors.

that the miners are playing honest, as we discussed earlier in this guide. So a small miner (operating a machine of modest power) will probably earn more by joining a mining pool with 100 other miners, rather than a mining pool with only 10 other miners.

However, even though the statement above is true (as of this writing), that doesn't mean the mining sector has a built-in drive to become one giant firm. The logic of spreading out the fixed overhead cost eventually tapers off. For example, even though the individual miner might perceive a clear advantage in joining a pool of 100 rather than 10 miners, he might *not* see much difference in expected earnings if the choice is between a pool of 10,000 miners versus 5,000.

In any case, at *no* scale is the expected solution rate *per hash* improved; it takes the same number of hashes (in expectation) to find a solution, regardless of whether a miner works alone or with a large pool. The intuition here is quite simple: If Amy has a modest computer devoted to mining, while Bill has a more powerful machine that can perform twice as many calculations per second, then over the course of a year we would expect Bill to earn twice as many bitcoins. This is what economists call *constant* returns to scale; there is no inherent tendency to agglomerate. When various miners link their individual (and weak) machines into one coordinated (and strong) pool, there is no computational reason for the *total* solutions produced by the group collectively to increase. Indeed, because the mining pool involves different people—some of whom may not be trustworthy—we might expect the total number of bitcoins earned by the group to be *lower* than if each machine worked in isolation, because the pool framework means that some of the computational power of the hardware must be devoted to "overhead" administrative tasks.

To repeat our discussion on mining pools from earlier in the guide, remember that the true rationale for joining a mining pool is that it "smoothens out" the expected payoff to the small miner. Depending on the strength of his equipment, a lone wolf miner might go months without ever receiving any bitcoins, but then all of a sudden hit paydirt. By joining a mining pool, the individual miner actually slightly *reduces* his or her expected payout (once we account for fees), but the payout is much more dependable because the group proceeds are distributed according to the relative contribution from each member.[54]

When considering the current size of various mining pools, we need to keep in mind that Bitcoin is a relatively new industry that has not attracted serious investment of computational power, compared to other sectors of the economy. Yet over time, as the cost of computational power continues to fall and (we might expect) the "market cap" of Bitcoin rises, we can expect to see continued investment in mining such that today's powerhouses (such as GHash) may continue to grow in absolute size but shrink relative to the network itself. Ultimately GHash and other potential "big players" will be kept in check *not* through pledges and the honor code, but through competition.

An analogy might help: Picture a suburb of a Midwestern city. At first, there is hardly a market for Thai cuisine; just a few immigrants from Thailand would buy such meals. In the beginning, one restaurant opens. For a while, it is the only authentic Thai place in town; it has a "natural monopoly" because of its "economies of scale." After all, if the market will only support (say) 100 Thai meals per week, then clearly it makes sense to concentrate their production all in one restaurant, because of the fixed overhead costs of renting the building, buying the right ingredients, printing up Thai menus, getting cooks who can prepare authentic recipes, etc. However, as the suburb's population grows over the years and its residents become more cosmopolitan, the demand for Thai food grows. At some point, a competitor opens a second restaurant, when it no longer makes sense to expand the operations of the

---

[54] A related advantage to individual miners from joining a mining pool is that the agreement effectively "locks in" the expected (bitcoin-denominated) return to mining at the current difficulty rate, hedging against a future in which their contributions might be effectively worthless (or, for that matter, against learning after years of mining that they had the configuration set up incorrectly).

original one. Down the road, when there are (say) a dozen Thai places around town, nobody would think to call it a "natural monopoly."

We expect to see a similar pattern unfold with mining pools in Bitcoin. Look, the people involved in Bitcoin aren't stupid; they can see—much more clearly than the outside critics—the danger of a giant mining pool. If the public at large doesn't trust the legitimacy and safety of the ledger, then it restricts the market for bitcoin holders and thus limits the potential value of an individual bitcoin. Individual miners will therefore have even a purely financial incentive—beyond their ideological commitment—to pull out of large mining pools and join smaller ones. Especially as the industry matures, such a move should carry not only long-range financial benefits (by promoting public trust), but should carry at most a negligible short-term dip in the expected earnings for the individual miner.

Before leaving this section, we should clarify the nature of what "corruption" would look like in the Bitcoin world. Right now, if the people running (say) PayPal or a commercial bank simply *lie* and take money from rightful owners and transfer it to themselves, the victims have an uphill battle. They would have to go to *other* third parties (like the Better Business Bureau or State agencies) and demand an investigation into the skullduggery. The process could take a long time, and if the corrupt bank officials were crafty enough, they might be able to hide what they did.

In complete contrast, if (say) the people running GHash decided to go rogue and double-spend bitcoins to benefit themselves, the rest of the network would realize what they were doing very quickly—the whole world would be onto their scheme within hours. And the accusations wouldn't rest on vague suspicions; it would be quite demonstrable what the rogue mining pool ringleaders had done, as their signatures would be on both sides of the double-spend, broadcast at the same time, originating from maximally-distant nodes on the network (so as to maximize the window in which they can get away with the goods they fraudulently purchased).[55] They might get away with a spending spree for a few hours, but then they would be ruined; the individual miners who were unwittingly involved with the scheme would pull out of such an unscrupulous organization. This last point is crucial to understanding the relatively fragile power of the people running a mining pool: Even though (with the current procedures) the leaders can assign tasks so that the individual miners don't see the "big picture," the only way the mining pool can command such strength is if the individual miners continue to follow orders. In our hypothetical scenario, once the individual miners realized they were helping to verify double-spends—a realization that would occur very quickly and then be noticed by a growing number of Bitcoin users[56]—these miners would withdraw from the pool, because *they* certainly don't benefit from helping other people rip off the community. The corrupt leaders would then only have their own hardware that they could directly control, which would be a drop in the bucket compared to the total computational power of the network.

Now after the individual miners pulled out of the pool, the wave of double-spends would cease. What would be the lasting effect of this traumatic episode? Beyond the losses of those who had been directly victimized in the wave of double-spending, everyone else holding bitcoins would probably also suffer, as people tried to dump their bitcoins once trust in the protocol had been so severely challenged. When the dust settled, everyone in the Bitcoin community would have learned a valuable

---

[55] For an analogy, it would be as if the people running a top mathematics journal published an invalid "proof" to benefit their buddy. Once a single reader noticed the problem and raised the alarm, the entire mathematical community would quickly agree that the result was invalid and the journal editors would be ruined.

[56] It's difficult to answer the question of how long it would take before a mining pool (which was composed of individually moral miners but run by an unscrupulous ringleader) would collapse after the initial wave of double-spends commenced. Notice that this isn't merely a technical question: Even after a certain fraction of the miners knew what was going on, others might be asleep or in a movie theater. Because of practical issues such as these, we are saying the initially dominant mining pool would collapse "within a few hours" just to avoid overstatement.

lesson after such a spanking—much like what happened with Mt. Gox—and would be much more sensitive to the danger of joining an already-dominant mining pool.

To be clear, we don't *predict* that the above will happen. On the contrary, we've explained why we think the worries over a "natural monopoly" in mining pools will fade away over the years, as the industry grows and its "lumpiness" is flattened out.[57] Our point in the above narrative was to show that even in a worst-case scenario, it's not as if the rogue mining pool would exercise power indefinitely over the hapless victims—the outlaw outfit would be identified as a bunch of criminals and would topple from their position within a few hours. Precisely *because* of this fact, the management of large mining pools might decide that—morality aside—it made more sense to continue playing by the rules, since that arguably would be more profitable in the long run.[58]

---

[57] In a way, Bitcoin has already gone through cycles in which previously-dominant mining technologies were eclipsed as more capital was invested in mining. In the very beginning, people could use their ordinary computers to mine, but these were made obsolete when users pressed high-end graphics cards into service as miners, which in turn were surpassed by FPGA pools, and later ASICs (circuits designs specifically for Bitcoin).

[58] Because this particular objection has been advanced as an "economic" one— where normal market forces allegedly would destroy Bitcoin from within—we have answered it in kind. However, it's conceivable that outsiders with a desire to destroy the Bitcoin network would work by building up an "innocent" mining pool and then engaging in a massive double-spending attack. (The players in such a scenario could be agents of various States or traditional banking interests, for example, who feel threatened by the promise of Bitcoin and other crypto-currencies.) Our response to this type of concern is the same as what we've put in the text above, although admittedly the fact that such a gambit would probably be unprofitable in terms of bitcoins would not be a deterrent for such rogues.

December 2014

VII. Conclusion

We hope this guide has provided you with the framework to understand Bitcoin from the perspectives of both economic theory and cryptography. In short, we hope that you now really understand what Bitcoin *is* and how it works.

In closing, let us remind you of the three caveats we provided upfront. First, we are NOT recommending Bitcoin as an investment. Naturally, our guide will help readers make a more informed decision, but we are not here making any prediction about the market value of bitcoins relative (say) to State-issued currencies over the next few years.

Second, we have focused on the specific example of Bitcoin, but keep in mind that there are many other crypto-currencies. Much of the framework we developed for Bitcoin would be applicable to them (perhaps with minor tweaks), but it's important to realize that Bitcoin itself could conceivably fade into obscurity if and when superior protocols are introduced.

Finally, we heartily encourage people to distribute this free guide to other interested readers. We only ask that proper attribution is given to Silas Barta and Robert P. Murphy, and that distributors occasionally check the website http://understandingbitcoin.us to make sure that they have the latest version of the guide.

December 2014

Hey!

How bout a little something, you know, for the effort?

If you found this guide helpful, we heartily encourage you to explore the ease of Bitcoin's payment system firsthand by sending us contributions. Each of the Bitcoin addresses below goes to one of the authors. (We flipped a coin to determine whether Barta or Murphy's would be first.) Thanks!

← 1B49UVtAwFHvtdMMVvzsBHrMrCsdCcdS8C

← 12rQwL3ozuZ7e8RV3Njfs3PLohgtA3Z1Vz

Works Cited

Dimand, Robert W. (1999) "Irving Fisher and the Fisher Relation: Setting the Record Straight," *The Canadian Journal of Economics*, Vol. 32, No. 3 (May 1999), pp. 744-750.

Ebeling, Richard (ed.). ([1978] 1996) *The Austrian Theory of the Trade Cycle and Other Essays* (Auburn, AL: Mises Institute), available at: https://mises.org/library/austrian-theory-trade-cycle-and-other-essays

Hayek, Friedrich. ([1976] 1990) *Denationalisation of Money: The Argument Refined: An Analysis of the Theory and Practice of Concurrent Currencies* (London: The Institute of Economic Affairs), available at: http://mises.org/sites/default/files/Denationalisation%20of%20Money%20The%20Argument%20Refined_5.pdf.

Jones, Charles. (2009) "Consumption," Chapter 20 of a textbook discussion hosted at Stanford website, available at: http://web.stanford.edu/~chadj/Consumption2009-11-25.pdf.

Klein, Benjamin. (1974) "The Competitive Supply of Money," *Journal of Money, Credit, and Banking*, Vol. 6, 1974, November, pp. 523-553.

Krugman, Paul. (2013) "Bits and Barbarism," *The New York Times*, December 22, 2013, available at http://www.nytimes.com/2013/12/23/opinion/krugman-bits-and-barbarism.html.

Lara, Carlos and Robert P. Murphy. (2010) *How Privatized Banking Really Works* (Ann Arbor, Michigan) available at: http://consultingbyrpm.com/uploads/HPBRW.pdf

Mises, Ludwig von. ([1912] 1953) *The Theory of Money and Credit* (New Haven, Yale University Press), available at: http://mises.org/library/theory-money-and-credit

Murphy, Robert P. (2003) "Unanticipated Intertemporal Change in Theories of Interest," May 2003, NYU doctoral dissertation, available at: http://consultingbyrpm.com/uploads/Dissertation.pdf.
———(2003) "The Origins of Money and Its Value," September 29, 2003, Mises Daily article, available at: http://mises.org/daily/1333
———(2005) "Hayek's Plan for Private Money," Mises Daily Article, July 18, 2005, available at: http://mises.org/library/hayeks-plan-private-money
———(2006) *Study Guide* to Murray Rothbard's *Man, Economy, and State with Power and Market* (Auburn, AL: Mises Institute), available at: http://mises.org/library/study-guide-man-economy-and-state
———(2007) *The Politically Incorrect Guide to Capitalism* (Washington, DC: Regnery)
———(2010) "The Fed as Giant Counterfeiter," February 1, 2010, Mises Daily article, available at: https://mises.org/library/fed-giant-counterfeiter
———(2010) *Lessons for the Young Economist* (Auburn, AL: Mises Institute), available at: http://mises.org/library/lessons-young-economist
———(2011) *Study Guide* to Ludwig von Mises' *Theory of Money and Credit* (Auburn, AL: Mises Institute), available at: http://mises.org/library/study-guide-theory-money-and-credit
———(2012) "Origin of the Specie," The American Conservative, April 11, 2012, available at: http://www.theamericanconservative.com/articles/origin-of-the-specie/.
——— (2013) "The Economics of Bitcoin," June 3, 2013, EconLib Featured Article, available at: http://www.econlib.org/library/Columns/y2013/Murphybitcoin.html.

Nakamoto, Satoshi (2008). "Bitcoin: A Peer-to-Peer Electronic Cash System," November 2008, available at: https://bitcoin.org/bitcoin.pdf.

Pittman, Mark. (2008) "Fed Refuses to Disclose Recipients of $2 Trillion," Bloomberg News, December 12, 2008, available at: http://www.bloomberg.com/apps/news?pid=newsarchive&sid=aGvwttDayiiM

Rothbard, Murray. ([1962] 2009) *Man, Economy, and State, With Power and Market* (Scholar's Edition, 2nd edition), available at: http://mises.org/document/1082/Man-Economy-and-State-with-Power-and-Market
————([1962] 2001) *The Case for a 100 Percent Gold Dollar* (Auburn, AL: Mises Institute), available at: http://mises.org/sites/default/files/Case%20for%20a%20100%20Percent%20Gold%20Dollar_2.pdf.
————([1983] 2008) *The Mystery of Banking*, 2nd edition (Auburn, AL: Mises Institute), available at: http://mises.org/library/mystery-banking-1

Selgin, George. (1999) "A Plea for (Mild) Deflation," Cato Policy Report, May/June 1999, Vol. 21, No. 3, available at: http://www.cato.org/sites/cato.org/files/serials/files/policy-report/1999/5/cpr-21n3.html.
——— (2011) *Good Money: Birmingham Button Makers, the Royal Mint, and the Beginnings of Modern Coinage, 1775-1821* (Oakland, CA: The Independent Institute).

Šurda, Peter. (2014) "The origin, classification, and utility of Bitcoin." Paper presented at the Austrian Economics Research Conference (AERC) 2014 in Auburn, Alabama.

Tucker, Jeffrey. (2014) *Bit By Bit: How P2P Is Freeing the World* (Liberty.me).

About the Authors

Silas Barta works as a software developer in San Francisco and has been involved in several Bay Area startups. He first learned of Bitcoin while role-playing the problem of how non-human intelligences would interact with the global financial system despite lacking citizenship, after which he built a liquid-cooled mining rig from off-the-shelf graphics cards. Prior to that, Silas worked as an aerospace engineer in Texas. He has been active for years in discussions of how traditional State functions could be replaced by stateless alternatives. He blogs, and promotes mouseless interaction with computers, at http://blog.tyrannyofthemouse.com and can be reached at sbarta@gmail.com.

Robert P. Murphy is an economist specializing in free-market education of the intelligent layperson. He has a PhD in economics from New York University and spent three years teaching at Hillsdale College. In 2006 Murphy left academia for the financial sector. He is currently the Senior Economist for the Institute for Energy Research (IER) and a research fellow with the Independent Institute. Murphy has testified before Congress on several occasions and is a frequent guest on radio and TV outlets. He is the author of numerous books, including *The Politically Incorrect Guide to Capitalism* (Regnery 2007), *Lessons for the Young Economist* (Mises Institute 2010, available at: http://mises.org/library/lessons-young-economist), and the *Study Guide* to Ludwig von Mises' *Theory of Money and Credit* (Mises Institute 2011, available at: http://mises.org/library/study-guide-theory-money-and-credit). Murphy runs the blog "Free Advice" located at: www.ConsultingByRPM.com. He can be contacted at rpm@ConsultingByRPM.com.

www.ingramcontent.com/pod-product-compliance
Lightning Source LLC
Chambersburg PA
CBHW051814170526
45167CB00005B/2010